Praise for Deb Hornell's
Good Things for a Full Life

This book provides a practical, hands-on roadmap to achieving a full life. Deb Hornell has a unique way of blending the sound fundamentals of good business planning with the use of real-life examples. For over a decade, I've witnessed her application of this formula in developing hundreds of female executives. Throughout the many years I've known Deb, she has asked the right questions; coached me on the answers; and constantly urged me to do more. And now, others can benefit from her expertise by reading this great book.

TONY HUNTER, CEO, TRIBUNE PUBLISHING
AND CEO AND PUBLISHER, CHICAGO TRIBUNE COMPANY

A book on "Good Things for a Full Life" is good. The fact that it is written by Deb Hornell makes it great. Deb has focused her career (and life) on figuring out how to make her life and the lives of others better. Deb has a unique perspective on how to maintain a healthy balance in life and how that balance is the key to personal and professional fulfillment. This book will be its best not when read but when practiced!

BOB MARSHALL, VICE PRESIDENT US OPERATIONS, MCDONALD'S CORPORATION

Throughout "Good Things for a Full Life," Deb Hornell draws on her own professional and personal experiences and success, inspiring and enabling others to create their own full and satisfying lives. Deb's unique perspective and sense of humor comes through in every story, and her probing questions provide a roadmap for taking action. This is a book that, if you are willing to do the work recommended, can help lead you to achieving good things for your full life, regardless of your age or situation.

JEAN OTTE, FOUNDER OF WOMEN UNLIMITED, INC.

To put it simply, Deb Hornell has always inspired me. She is in the rarified league of people who consistently, consciously, and clearly live a life that is fully aligned with their stated values and intentions. Even more importantly, she is the person I can count on to ask great questions and to provide insightful, yet ultimately practical advice. With this book, Deb can now inspire you to be more intentional, to reflect ("What's that about?!"), and to live a full life.

AMY GONZALES, FOUNDER AND PRESIDENT, AG LEADERSHIP

Deb Hornell's philosophy is not about having it all, but deciding what matters. In the many years I have known Deb, I've watched her engage with her family, her work, many volunteer causes, her faith, graduate school, and regular exercise. "Good Things for a Full Life" provides tips, anecdotes, and reflections to help prioritize what we want instead of just letting life happen.

Amy Hohulin, Amy Hohulin Training & Development

I have known and worked with Deb Hornell for over 15 years. During that time, she has been an inspiration to me personally and an inspiration to many women within our company. Deb has a way of telling it like it is, so this book will be a refreshing approach to helping readers lead a full life.

Patricia Brown James, Vice President, Shared Services Division,
Bridgestone Americas, Inc.

Accomplished and real. That is what Deb Hornell is and why her new book, "Good Things for a Full Life," is perfect for anyone who has a need for something else in life—regardless of how big or small. Deb is the role model of creating good things in life. Her ability to define what she wants and her process for making it happen have provided Deb with many good things along her journey. Let her model draw you closer to your good life!

Susan Kendrick, Founder of highwirecoach.com™ and Bowser College Inc.™

Many books today present concepts that, although interesting, are often difficult to put into practice. Deb Hornell's book has a wealth of suggestions—good things—each of which is actionable and will make a difference in your life and the life of others. It is simply up to the reader to choose. If you see an idea that you think is commonplace, just remember that it is probably not common practice! This little gem has a wealth of ideas that can be used immediately. No special skill is required, just a willingness to be at your best. Applying just one of the suggestions will recharge you and provide deep, meaningful improvement for your spiritual, personal, professional and physical life. Go ahead, be more effective and start today to achieve your full life, beginning with chapter one!

Bob Roberts, Ph.D., Strategic Organization Development,
Texas Health Resources

Across industries, business conditions, and personal career choices, I have come to depend on Deb Hornell for advice and feedback. She is a facilitator supreme, whose acumen is based on "know thyself" and how to link your personal and professional goals to the world you live in. You now have the opportunity to share in what my friend of 25 years has shared with me: The key to a life of satisfaction and joy is in pursuing your personal objectives.

Rick Surkamer, President of Surkamer Advisers, LLC

GOOD THINGS

for a Full Life

BY DEB HORNELL

ISBN 978-1481923545

DEDICATION

To Glorya
my friend, my mentor, my role model for a full life

FORWARD

by Laura Sanchez-Greenberg

You hold in your hands something you've been looking for.

The universe delivers to us just what we need, exactly how we need it. This book, whether in its entirety or in a single chapter, will deliver what you need.

There are people and events that help us find our true selves and choose our true paths—to live our fullest lives. Deb Hornell has been that person for me and countless others over the past 25 years of her career. In so many ways, she has shared what we lovingly call her "Deb-ness" at the right time, in the right way. Like a candle lighting hundreds of flames, Deb has inspired many to live fuller lives. Those many have gone out to light other flames, changing lives in little and big ways, simply by realizing that anything is possible. These collective flames now form a raging fire, and you will soon feel its warmth in your hands.

I encourage you to read this book, take what you need, share what you love, and join all of us in enjoying *Good Things for a Full Life*.

Laura Sanchez-Greenberg is changing the world as Senior Vice President at New Futuro, mother to two fabulous boys, wife, mentor, friend, sister, daughter, adventurer, and long-time friend and follower of Deb Hornell.

ACKNOWLEDGEMENTS

They say it takes a village to raise a child.
There's a large village I want to thank for raising me!

- My parents, Paul and Sallie Andresen, my first teachers, for fostering my values and work ethic; and my four brothers, Dave, Bruce, Doug, and Mike for making me a strong woman. You all gave me a foundation and launched me into the world.
- My husband Bill, who is my partner in our blessed life together; our children Laura, Lindsay, and Matt; my son-in-law Phil; and my dog Abby, who all hold me accountable for practicing what I preach. You are my rock and bring me such joy.
- My mother-in-law Glorya, who was my greatest mentor and role model in living a successful life. You were always one of my biggest cheerleaders.
- My large and diverse extended family, made up of Andresens, Smeads, Hornells, Matthews, and Yudys. You've all given me so many good memories and so much love.
- My spiritual leaders, Bob Cassell, Ken Stenman, Sheri Delvin, Jim Honig, and Heidi Johns, for nurturing my faith and challenging me to take my ministry into the world.
- Jean Otte, the founder of WOMEN Unlimited, Inc. for mentoring me and including me in her vision.
- Many friends and colleagues, especially my golf group, the OD Chicks, my WOMEN Unlimited colleagues, my Amelia sisters, Rebecca Wildeisen-Ehrke, Bob Sitze, and Kymme Lightfoot.
- Laura Sanchez-Greenberg for suggesting that I write a book and encouraging me to go for it.
- My incredible book/platform team who challenged me to think big while gently guiding me through the process: Beth Nyland, my writing coach and editor who also served as fearless leader of the team; Liz Abrams and Leslie Levine, the dynamic duo of social media and public relations; graphic designer Lee Roesner, who so elegantly conveyed the essence of my vision in the website and book design; Jim Nyland, who captured beautiful photographs and video; and my daughter Laura Yudys, who provided structure for the book and overall perspective and advice.
- My friends, colleagues, and family members who shared their stories as featured writers for various chapters: Beth Nyland, Maria Moore, Kymme Lightfoot, Laura Yudys, Doug Andresen, Bud Hornell, John Weaver, Catherine Lanucha, Nancy Hoying, Brenda Knapp, Bruce Andresen, Judy Busby, Bob Sitze, Deana Gelino, Gina Flaig, and Tamara Fay.

TABLE OF CONTENTS

Introduction 1

SECTION ONE:
GOOD THINGS FOR YOUR SPIRIT

Chapter 1: Strive for a full life, not balance 7
Chapter 2: Believe in something bigger than yourself 11
Chapter 3. Envision your legacy 15
Chapter 4: Be in the moment while keeping the end goal in mind . . . 19
Chapter 5: Pay attention to your words 23
Chapter 6: Everybody puts their pants on the same way, one leg at a time . 27
Chapter 7: What's your biggest fear? 31
Chapter 8: What's that about? 35
Chapter 9: With privilege comes responsibility 39
Chapter 10: Act your way to a new way of thinking. 43
Chapter 11: Your words and actions impact the words and actions of others . 47
Chapter 12: Someone needs to be the big person, how about you? 51
Chapter 13: Choices beget choices 55
Chapter 14: No regrets. 59

SECTION TWO:
GOOD THINGS FOR YOUR PERSONAL LIFE

Chapter 15: Your life as a chapter book 65
Chapter 16: No limits. 69
Chapter 17: Embrace decade transitions. 73
Chapter 18: Be a life-long learner 77
Chapter 19: Practice bucket management 81
Chapter 20: Turn off technology and tune into the world around you. . 85
Chapter 21: Parents: be clear on your role and don't lose yourself
            in the process. 89
Chapter 22: Mealtime is an opportunity to nourish your body
            and your relationships 93
Chapter 23: Be true to yourself and others. 97
Chapter 24: You can do anything you put your mind to 101
Chapter 25: The power of commitment 105

SECTION THREE:
GOOD THINGS FOR YOUR PROFESSIONAL LIFE

Chapter 26: Know what you bring to the table 111
Chapter 27: Create a yearly IDP and work that plan. 115
Chapter 28: Effort = ROI. 119
Chapter 29: Be more childlike and less childish at work 123
Chapter 30: Bring solutions, not excuses 127
Chapter 31: Be a bad ass, not a hard ass 131
Chapter 32: The only person you can really manage is yourself. 135
Chapter 33: Leadership is about behavior, not a title. 139
Chapter 34: In the absence of authority, people look for leadership . . . 143
Chapter 35: When you step aside, you allow someone else to step
             into a position of leadership 147
Chapter 36: Networking is about building connections, not
             collecting business cards 151
Chapter 37: Know what to ask for, and ask for more 155
Chapter 38: Always have a back-up plan 159

SECTION FOUR:
GOOD THINGS FOR YOUR PHYSICAL LIFE

Chapter 39: Practice self-care 165
Chapter 40: Despite your best intentions, stuff happens. 169

Contributors 173
Sources 179

INTRODUCTION

When my son Matt was in elementary school, he introduced the concept of "good things" as part of our nightly dinner table conversation. Each person had to say one good thing that had happened that day. "Good things" became an important family tradition. Although some balked when it was their turn, we began to appreciate the opportunity to connect with and learn more about each other. Because we knew we'd have to report to the family each night, we intentionally looked for "good things" each day, and that fostered in all of us a positive outlook on life. So Matt gets credit for giving us a healthy discipline, and for the title of this book.

Positivity is a big part of who I am. Some might say I've had a charmed life. While I am grateful for my many blessings, I firmly believe that my good fortune has not come through sheer luck. I have made choices, honored commitments, and been humble in asking for feedback and help.

So, when I began to think about what it takes to have a full and satisfying life, I realized that there are people and principles that have shaped my thinking and approach. This is the substance of the personal and leadership development workshops I facilitate as part of my consulting business. And now it is also the core content of this book.

None of what you will encounter in these pages is earth shattering. It's just commonsense stuff that works.

Good Things for a Full Life is based on the framework I use to create a yearly Individual Development Plan (IDP)—for myself as well as for the professionals I coach. My framework includes sections common to many development plan formats: an overarching theme for the year; goals and actions aligned with that theme; individuals who will serve as accountability partners for goals; and milestones/measurements.

What makes the *Good Things for a Full Life* framework unique is that we categorize goals into four distinct areas of focus:

- Good Things for Your Spirit: goals and actions to feed the spirit, such as creative and artistic activities, volunteer activities, and religious endeavors (if applicable)
- Good Things for Your Personal Life: goals and actions to deepen relationships with family and friends
- Good Things for Your Professional Life: work-related goals and actions to enhance career results and satisfaction
- Good Things for Your Physical Life: goals and actions related to self-care and health

Throughout the book, you'll see the repeated image of a tree, which illustrates how these four elements work together in a full life. Good Things for Your Spirit are represented by the roots of the tree, as a healthy spirit is necessary to feed and support all the other areas. The Personal, Professional, and Physical aspects of a full life are shown in the lush foliage of the tree's canopy—where we bear fruit and grow upward and outward over time.

My hope, as you read and reflect on *Good Things for a Full Life*, is that you will find a few items that make sense and inspire you to take action to create a full and satisfying life for yourself. Each chapter starts with a headline I commonly use when coaching others. (My friends and family members have heard some of these one-liners so often, they occasionally toss them back at me.) Under the headline you'll find an image or a short reflection by someone who's been an important part of my life. Next, you'll find a few paragraphs from me, articulating the wisdom behind the headline. And finally, each chapter closes with a series of "Good Questions" to challenge your thinking and nudge you to action.

Take your time. Read the chapters in order or pick and choose at random. I hope my examples and the insights from other contributors will spark your thinking about your own life. I hope you discover what a full life means to you and how you can be more intentional in creating that life for yourself.

Here are some ways to incorporate *Good Things for a Full Life* into your life:

- Read one chapter at a time, perhaps one each day or one each week. Reflect on the story, think about the questions, and answer them as honestly as you can.
- Read one section at a time. See what resonates with you. Highlight the key headlines or phrases that make sense.
- Read the book with a trusted friend or colleague, and discuss each headline and what it means to you.
- Visit our online community at hornellpartners.com to read our blog posts, read about others' experiences, or post your own ideas, successes, and challenges.
- Attend one of our virtual or in-person workshops to take advantage of additional exercises to create the framework for your own full life.
- Contact us to schedule a workshop for your company or networking group.

Let's go make *Good Things* happen!

SECTION ONE

GOOD THINGS
for Your Spirit

The *Oxford American Desk Dictionary and Thesaurus, 2nd edition*
defines spirit as "the animating essence of a person; a person's mental
or moral nature or qualities."

The chapters in this section speak to the core of who you are:

- Fundamental principles that influence how you interact in
  the world
- The stuff that feeds your soul

The headlines and stories contained in each chapter set a foundation for
living a full and satisfying life, while also applying to the other areas of a
full life: Personal, Professional, and Physical.

CHAPTER 1

STRIVE FOR A FULL LIFE, NOT BALANCE

Balance is a Myth
by Beth Nyland

*why do we seek
balance?
some mythical
symmetry
between
work and play
public and private
activity and rest?*

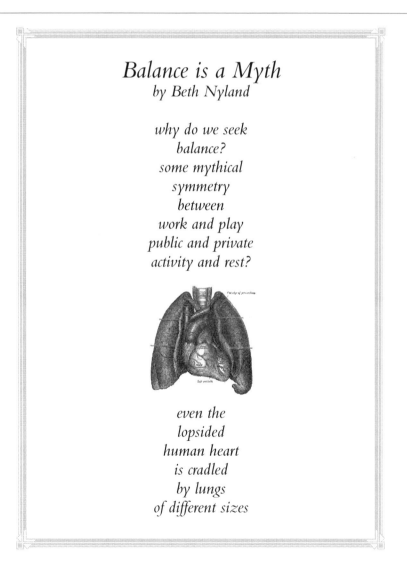

*even the
lopsided
human heart
is cradled
by lungs
of different sizes*

Around age 35, I began to focus on how I could manage the competing priorities in my life. Like so many others, I wondered if I would ever find "work-life balance."

I couldn't.

And neither can you. It simply is not realistic! In fact, this popular concept of "balancing" work and life sets us up for failure and frustration. It implies that work and life are somehow separate; they're not. It suggests that you can achieve perfect equilibrium between time at work and time outside work; you can't. It assumes that there is one "equation" that will work for you for your whole life; there isn't. As your life evolves, different parts of your life will hold greater weight over other areas.

Instead, consider what you want your life to be full of. Work? Family? Friends? Exercise? School? Volunteer activities? Travel? Something else? Make a list. Then, look at the list again. Is there anything you've forgotten? Is there something you love to do, but haven't had time for in awhile? Add it to your list.

Don't be content with a list that is heavily focused on just one item. Just as a financial advisor recommends diversifying investments to mitigate risk, you should diversify your activities to avoid investing too much in one area of your life. If you over-invest in one area, a loss there will hit you harder than if you have a more balanced "portfolio."

Think about the choices you make with regard to work. Are you the one who's always asked to stay late, finish others' tasks, or take on extra assignments? If you haven't given other priorities enough weight, you may have allowed work to take over your life, and will need to add other commitments that will pull you away from work. Join a gym or sign on with a personal trainer; volunteer somewhere; start a book or dinner club; take vacations.

Be sure it's your list—things that fulfill you, that nourish your spirit. Not what others need in their lives. Not an agenda dictated by how "they" think you should spend your time. Only you can determine what you need to be satisfied.

By choosing how to spend your time and energy, you will feel a greater sense of control over your life, experience more satisfaction, and be less reactive to the whims of others. You will be better prepared to weather the ups and downs of life. Your energy and satisfaction will not be tucked into an isolated pocket of work, home, or family, but shared across your full life.

GOOD QUESTIONS

1. What do you want your life to be full of? Why those things?

\
\
\
\
\
\
\
\
\
\
\
\

2. Are those things present in your life now? Why or why not?

\
\
\
\

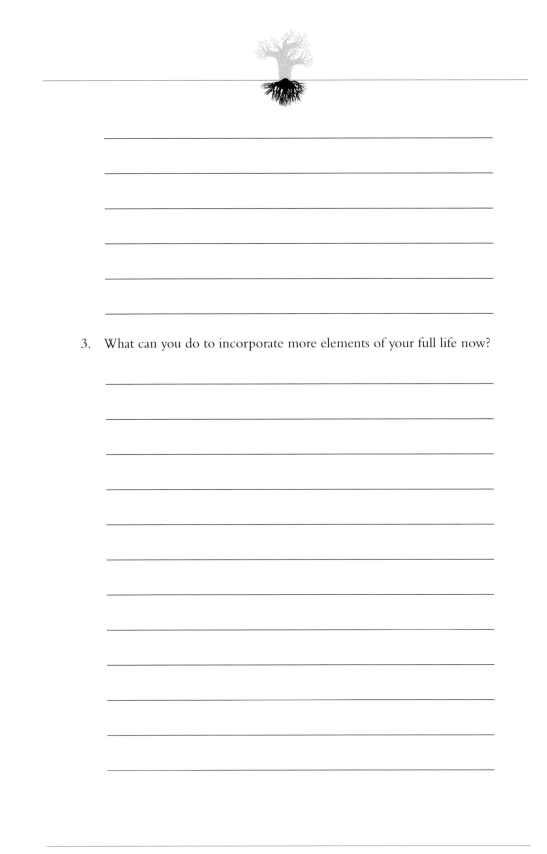

_____

_____

_____

_____

_____

_____

3. What can you do to incorporate more elements of your full life now?

_____

_____

_____

_____

_____

_____

_____

_____

_____

_____

_____

_____

GOOD THINGS
for Your Spirit

CHAPTER 2

BELIEVE IN SOMETHING
BIGGER THAN YOURSELF

A "speck on a speck in a speck." That's how Carl Sagan, author of the book and popular television mini-series documentary *Cosmos*, referred to the human population, describing our place in the universe. When I first heard that phrase, I was awestruck. It put into perspective that we are but a small part of something much grander than ourselves, that there are more important things than disposable material goods or the present moment in time.

Believe in something bigger than yourself. It doesn't matter what—a higher power, the earth, science, or the goodness of humanity. Just believe. And have respect for the beliefs of others, too.

GOOD QUESTIONS

1. What do you believe in? Why?

_____

_____

_____

_____

_____

_____

_____

_____

2. How do your beliefs guide your life and provide you with perspective?

_____

_____

_____

_____

_____

_____

_____

_____

_____

_____

_____

3. How has learning about other beliefs helped you accept others and open your mind to possibilities outside your own experience?

_____

_____

_____

_____

_____

_____

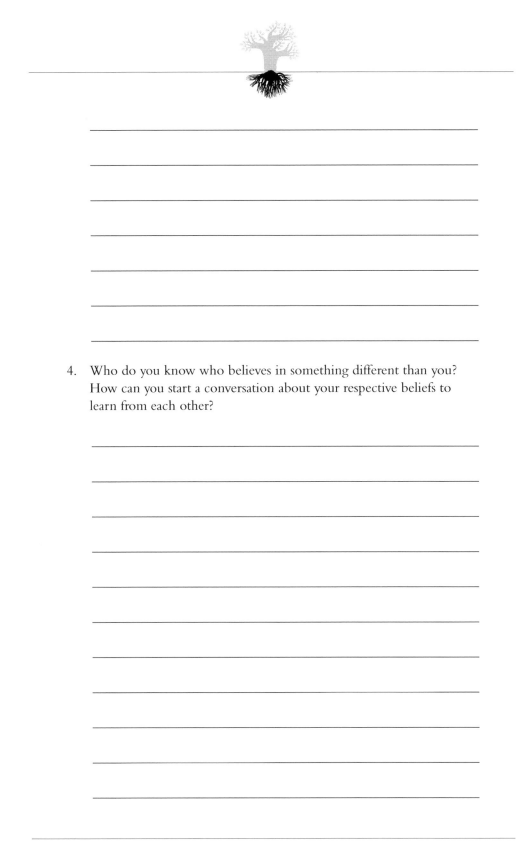

_____

_____

_____

_____

_____

_____

4. Who do you know who believes in something different than you? How can you start a conversation about your respective beliefs to learn from each other?

_____

_____

_____

_____

_____

_____

_____

_____

_____

_____

GOOD THINGS
for Your Spirit

CHAPTER 3

ENVISION YOUR LEGACY

"Aha" Moment
by Maria Moore

When you turn the page, you will learn about Deb's eightieth birthday exercise. This deceptively simple exercise forced me to rethink goals I had set early in my life.

Near the end of my thirties, having accomplished everything I had set out to do, I didn't care to look more than 40 years into the future. So when Deb challenged me to think about my eightieth birthday, I pushed back. I balked and pouted, and I told her I didn't want or need to do this work. Talk about denial!

What I needed was to embrace myself as a powerful woman and thoughtful leader. I did not realize what was to come as a result of doing this important work on myself.

After my adult tantrum, I did work through the exercise—though I planned for my fortieth birthday instead of my eightieth. As a result, my fortieth birthday celebration was purposeful and authentic. Over the course of that milestone year, I enjoyed moments that were external, exuberant, and vibrant, as well as others that were internal, quiet, and self-affirming.

Now I accept that I need to be present and aware of my own journey regardless of the context. I will continue to go forth and celebrate "me" as woman, daughter, sister, aunt, godmother, friend, lover, spiritual child, gardener, singer, traveler, mentor, and leader by choice and at every age.

Have you ever considered what you want your life to be about? What you want to be known for? The legacy you want to create?

One way to do this is to imagine yourself on your eightieth birthday.

I know what you're thinking: "I don't want to think of myself as elderly and frail, near the end my life."

So don't. There are no rules with this exercise, just imagination.

When I think of my eightieth birthday, I see myself looking and feeling the way I did as a beautiful, young woman of thirty-four (and I was hot!). My friends and family are gathered together for a three-day party on Martha's Vineyard, a beautiful island near Cape Cod—a favorite vacation spot that holds many happy memories for my family and me. The guests represent all aspects of my full life, including family, friends, colleagues, and spiritual leaders—people who have had a significant impact on me. We eat wonderful food, sing and dance a lot, share stories, and make new memories.

In my vision, the party-goers include even those who may not be alive when I turn eighty—people like my husband's grandparents, who graciously welcomed me to their family. They taught me a lot about marriage, parenting, and living an authentic life. No celebration of my life would be complete without them.

So don't worry about how you will look or what aches and pains may afflict you at age eighty. Instead, envision a celebration of your life, how you most wish to celebrate, who will honor you, and what they will appreciate about you.

By considering the people who matter to you and how your life touches them, you will define your legacy—what you want to be known for. Then you can make decisions and take action to live in ways that are true to that legacy.

GOOD QUESTIONS

1. How would you celebrate your milestone birthday?

   _____

   _____

   _____

   _____

   _____

2. Where are you? Why that place? What does that location represent to you?

   _____

   _____

   _____

   _____

   _____

3. Who is with you? Why those people? What do they mean to you?

   _____

   _____

   _____

   _____

_____

_____

_____

4. What are people saying about you? Why are their comments
    important to you?

    _____

    _____

    _____

    _____

    _____

5. How can you begin living and acting in ways that support your
    legacy? What activities and people need more attention? What
    activities and people need less attention?

    _____

    _____

    _____

    _____

    _____

    _____

GOOD THINGS
for Your Spirit

CHAPTER 4

BE IN THE MOMENT WHILE KEEPING THE END GOAL IN MIND

Hornell kids in 1992 and 2011

Many people stumble through life, reacting to events without a thought to where they are going or how their current actions affect the future. Not only are they failing to anticipate the future, they are missing opportunities to be fully present in the moment—to experience and appreciate the people and activities of their lives.

Although I am not a fan of football, it seems a fitting metaphor here. If you think about your life as a football game, what does winning mean to you? Who is on your team? Are you the quarterback of your full life—actively guiding the plays that will win the game—or are you waiting for a coach to tell you what to do? Are you relishing each play that moves you toward the end zone, or just rushing toward your victory dance?

Before I had children, I often thought about the kind of people I hoped to raise. Winning the parenting game for me meant two things: first, that my children would be responsible people, and second, that they would have a strong sense of self. Through the stages of their lives (and not all phases were easy!), I would ask myself this question:

"Is the way I'm interacting with my children right now
helping them to grow into the healthy, responsible adults I envision?"

If the answer was "no," I could self-correct. Like any good quarterback, I had to assess each situation and sometimes call a new play.

Even more challenging for me was taking time to enjoy each play, each step along the way. I was so busy organizing our lives—creating lists, running kids to activities, making sure people were fed—I often didn't stop long enough to enjoy the small moments. I had to continually tell myself to balance being in the current moment while keeping that vision of their future in mind. Although I cannot claim credit for the wonderful adults my children have become, I certainly am proud of my part in cultivating their growth. Our team has been able to win that game together, one play at a time.

We don't have the benefit of instant replay in our full lives; but we can take time-outs to assess our progress and call a new play if needed. By being thoughtful about your end goal and how you lead each play, you ensure that the actions you take and the relationships you build along the way will help you win the game.

GOOD QUESTIONS

1. What is your end goal (for yourself, for friends and family, for work, for your team, etc.)? Consider the legacy you are creating, to be celebrated at your eightieth birthday party.

    _____

    _____

    _____

    _____

    _____

    _____

    _____

    _____

    _____

    _____

2. Are you acting as the quarterback of your full life? Who is on your team? How are you calling plays? Are your actions moving you toward or diverting you away from your goal? What can you do to align your behavior and actions with the goal?

    _____

    _____

    _____

_____

_____

_____

_____

_____

_____

_____

_____

3. In what ways are you so busy that you may not be enjoying the individual moments of your life? What do you need to do to be more aware and present in the moment?

_____

_____

_____

_____

_____

_____

_____

_____

GOOD THINGS
for Your Spirit

CHAPTER 5

PAY ATTENTION TO YOUR WORDS

Powerful Listening
by Kymme Lightfoot

As I moved from the "corporate world" into the "consulting world," I assumed I would operate like most consultants I had worked with in the past, functioning as "the expert." I thought I had to have all the answers, that I needed to guide and direct, that clients expected me to fix their problems. Pretty haughty! Not surprisingly, the results did not always meet my expectations.

True to my lifelong belief in personal development, I dug deep to discover how I could thrive and be of service to my clients—to help them create the results they wanted, not the results I wanted for them. I realized I was allowing the noise around me, including my own expectations, to drive my actions. It wasn't until I quieted myself and listened that I began to hear answers.

Here's what I heard: I didn't have to be an over-the-top consultant. I could instead serve as a mirror to reflect back to clients what they present to the world. I could offer a safe place for them to express what they are capable of and where they could challenge their own thinking. My success as a consultant depends on my ability to be fully present and listen in different ways, to reflect on what I hear, and to give that gift of listening to my client. Changing my self-talk has put me on the path to realizing my true potential.

My friend Kymme is my accountability partner for my yearly business plan and my individual development plan. One year, while I was struggling to articulate a goal around a risky new business venture, Kymme stopped me.

"Listen to your words," she said.

I repeated what I had said. The gist was that I was defining my business and my successes through the lens of just one brand—and it wasn't even mine. My identity had become so entwined with one of my clients that people didn't remember or recognize my own company's name. What's more, even I was embracing this limited perspective. All this was keeping me from pushing my own business into an area of much-needed growth.

The story I told Kymme—and the very words I used to tell it—kept me from seeing beyond "what is" to "what could be." Kymme showed me that I was limiting myself through my own language. She explained that we often create barriers for ourselves with words like "I'll try" or "I can't" or "My client won't let me" or "I hate my boss."

Pay attention to the words coming out of your mouth. You just might discern how you feel about a person or situation. You might learn exactly what's holding you back.

Then you can begin crafting a new story: "I am" or "I can" or "My approach with my client is to …" or "I support my boss by … "

Once you change the words you use about a person or situation, you can envision new possibilities and feel greater commitment to making them happen.

GOOD QUESTIONS

1. Record yourself or have a trusted friend or colleague listen to you explain a challenging goal or person or situation.
    a) What words do you use?

    _____

    _____

    _____

    _____

    _____

    _____

    b) How do those words affect your commitment to the goal? Do your words make it difficult to imagine getting to a place of success?

    _____

    _____

    _____

    _____

    _____

    _____

    _____

2. Now rewrite your story about this goal or person or situation.
    a) What words will you use now?

    _____

    _____

    _____

    _____

    _____

    b) How do those words affect your commitment to the goal? Do
    your words make it easier to imagine getting to a place of success?

    _____

    _____

    _____

    _____

    _____

3. Now record yourself or have a trusted colleague listen to you tell the
    new story. Do you hear a difference? Do you believe it?

    _____

    _____

    _____

    _____

    _____

EVERYBODY PUTS THEIR PANTS ON THE SAME WAY: ONE LEG AT A TIME

My mother was a compassionate person, open to people of all races and creeds. As I was growing up, she would often say this phrase:

"Everybody puts their pants on the same way: one leg at a time."

You can interpret this two ways, both of them valuable:

- Don't ever think you are better than other people.
- Don't ever let yourself believe that others are better than you.

My mom's faith led her to believe that everyone is a "child of God." Even if you don't share her religious beliefs, you can appreciate the human desire to be known by and connected to others. Isn't it both humbling and comforting to know that we all put pants on just one leg at a time?

How you think and feel about yourself in relation to other people affects your relationships with others and with yourself.

Judging others—whether we put them on a pedestal or demean them— keeps us from accepting them for who they are. Judgment builds an emotional wall that prevents us from opening up to full, honest relationships. And when judgment leaks out of that wall, it often takes the ugly form of gossip or criticism.

So when you feel judgment creeping into your head, or hear yourself gossiping about or criticizing someone else, check yourself. Turn it around so you can be open to the other person and see him or her as my mother would—not better than you, not less than you, just different. Someone who puts pants on the same way you do: one leg at a time.

GOOD QUESTIONS

1. Are there people you believe are better than you? Who are they? What about them makes you feel inferior? How does that keep you from connecting with them as fellow human beings?

_____

_____

_____

_____

_____

_____

2. Do you think of yourself as better than others? Why? What need does that fill for you? How can you let go of that feeling to be more accepting of others?

_____

_____

_____

_____

_____

_____

3. Think about a time when you judged someone else. What did you think or say? How did that affect your relationship with the other person?

_____

_____

_____

_____

_____

_____

_____

_____

4. What can you do to check yourself when you feel judgment creeping into your head, or leaking out as gossip or criticism?

_____

_____

_____

_____

_____

_____

_____

WHAT'S YOUR BIGGEST FEAR?

Glorya passing on a little "advice" the day
before Deb's wedding.

My beloved mother-in-law, Glorya, was my mentor, friend, and role model for almost thirty-nine years. Because of her success as wife, mother, and businesswoman, I often asked her advice when faced with a challenge at work or home. She would ask me questions and patiently listen. Then, at some point, she would ask me this question:

"What is your biggest fear in this situation?"

Because I heard this question every time, I always knew it was coming. I knew that I would have to "fess up." Yet I always turned to her, ready to be asked.

Sure, I could have asked myself this question. But going to Glorya made it harder to hide from my fear. I trusted her to listen, without judgment. She helped me do three things:

- Articulate my fear.
- Determine how to prevent the feared result from happening.
- Plan how to manage myself if the feared result did happen.

Naming my fear enabled me to diffuse its power, and helped me create a strategy to prevent it from happening or to deal with it if it came true.

It takes courage to examine your fears. By asking yourself this question or having a trusted person guide your thinking, you can diffuse the power that fears hold over you.

GOOD QUESTIONS

1. What's your biggest fear? Why?

    _____

    _____

    _____

    _____

    _____

    _____

    _____

    _____

    _____

    _____

2. What actions can you take to prevent it from happening?

    _____

    _____

    _____

    _____

    _____

    _____

    _____

3. What actions can you take to deal with it if it does happen?

_____

_____

_____

_____

_____

_____

_____

_____

4. Who can be your Glorya—the person you trust to ask you this question?

_____

_____

_____

_____

_____

_____

_____

_____

GOOD THINGS
for Your Spirit

CHAPTER 8

WHAT'S THAT ABOUT?

The Miracle Question
by Deb Hornell

My husband and I have been married a long time. He knows every hot button I have. Sometimes he pushes them just to get a reaction or stir up a little excitement. I remember this particular episode like it was yesterday...

It was that awful time of day I refer to as the "witching hour"—that transition between work and non-work activities when everyone is tired and hungry. While standing at the stove preparing dinner, I spied Bill coming into the kitchen. He stopped right next to me and began talking (complaining?) about something. I don't remember what he said, but I do remember the emotion and tone with which he said it.

My typical response would have been to respond quickly and with the same level of emotion and tone Bill was directing at me. But this time I decided to try a question I had learned from my friend Rebecca. I stopped stirring, turned to Bill, and calmly said, "You've got a lot of emotion around this. What's that about?"

He stopped, looked at me, and said, "I have absolutely no idea," and walked right out of the kitchen!

I stood there, dumbfounded, trying to understand what had just happened. I also decided that Rebecca must be the most brilliant person in the world. Best of all, I learned that I could avoid escalating a non-important issue by simply asking a question.

To this day, I often hear Bill ask himself that same question when he's trying to figure something out. I just smile and walk away.

Once, while describing a challenging work situation to my friend Rebecca, I began to tear up. She stopped me, saying:

"You've got some emotion around this issue. What's that about?"

Rebecca's simple yet powerful question stopped me short. I struggled to figure out where the emotion came from. I realized my feelings had taken over, and I was no longer thinking objectively or logically. I was operating from emotion.

The question, "What's that about?" jolted me out of that emotional state into a place of objectivity. With Rebecca's help, I was able to examine the obstacles and create a plan to resolve the issue.

Since that day, I have uttered this question countless times—often to myself, and also to others. Either way, it is an incredibly useful tool.

When you feel your own emotions taking over, ask yourself, "What is this about?" Just a few moments of reflection will likely generate an answer. Once you know where the emotion is coming from, you can determine a way through it or around it.

Asking the question of, or even about, another person is a helpful way to avoid getting swept up in a wave of someone else's emotion and possibly crashing into the surf. When you encounter a person who is exhibiting strong emotion, you can:

- Ask yourself, "I wonder what that is about?" Thinking about the question detaches you from the emotion, while enabling you to actively listen to understand where he or she is coming from.
- Ask the question of the other person, like Rebecca did for me. "You've got some emotion about this topic. What's that about?" Recognize the risks before you speak; your intentions must be sincere and your delivery supportive—never sarcastic or condescending—or you will make the situation worse.

Imagine: A single question that can awaken your awareness about your own role in a situation and help you understand another person's point of view. That's a good one!

GOOD QUESTIONS

1. How can you use this question to check your own emotions?

_____

_____

_____

_____

_____

_____

_____

_____

_____

2. How can you use this question to understand others better?

_____

_____

_____

_____

_____

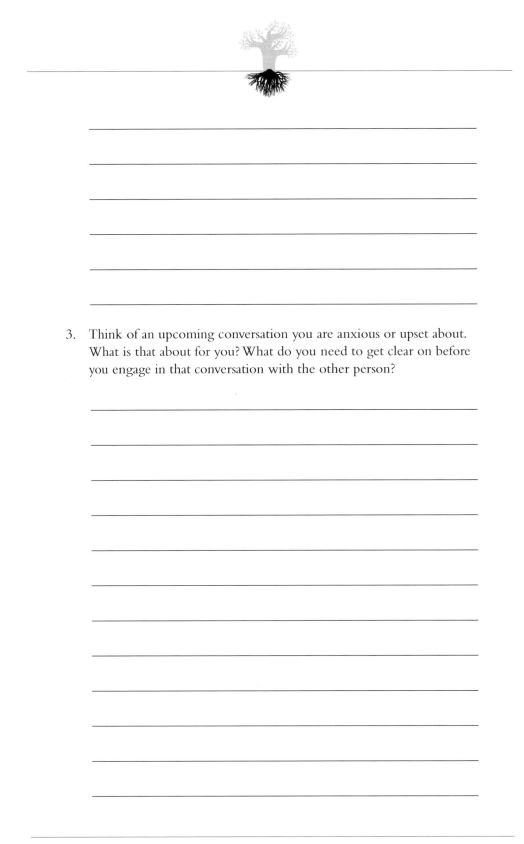

_____

_____

_____

_____

_____

_____

3. Think of an upcoming conversation you are anxious or upset about. What is that about for you? What do you need to get clear on before you engage in that conversation with the other person?

_____

_____

_____

_____

_____

_____

_____

_____

_____

_____

_____

_____

WITH PRIVILEGE
COMES RESPONSIBILITY

Andresen family in 1969 and 2009

As one of five children in a blue-collar family, I do not come from a wealthy background. We were not "privileged" with the sorts of extras and amenities affluent families enjoy. We rarely ate at restaurants, we didn't take family vacations, and we always shopped for sale items rather than paying full price.

Still, I was raised to appreciate the riches our family did have: parents who loved and nurtured us, musical and athletic abilities, intelligence, and faith. These were our privileges.

My parents, especially my father, encouraged me not to waste my talents, but to use them fully and purposefully. I was expected to complete a college degree, do meaningful work, participate in extracurricular activities, and actively serve others in my community.

My husband and I have been very blessed in our life together, fortunate to offer our children material comforts as well as more intangible benefits of a healthy, loving home and family. In turn, we expect our children to be responsible with those privileges—to use their education and talents for good, to nurture relationships with family and friends, to care for the environment, and to give of themselves to those less fortunate without expecting something in return.

Are you fixated on what's missing or in limited supply in your life? That kind of deficit thinking creates fear and prevents you from appreciating the world around you. Think instead about the privileges you have been given—the abundance of your full life. Then you can take stock of how those privileges have helped to shape your life—and maybe even how your areas of "lack" can actually make you stronger. Better yet, you may identify ways to give back or "pay it forward" to others.

GOOD QUESTIONS

1. What privileges have you been given in your life: talents, resources, family, friends, etc.?

    _____

    _____

    _____

    _____

    _____

    _____

    _____

    _____

    _____

2. What have you done to use those privileges wisely? When have you wasted or used them frivolously?

    _____

    _____

    _____

    _____

    _____

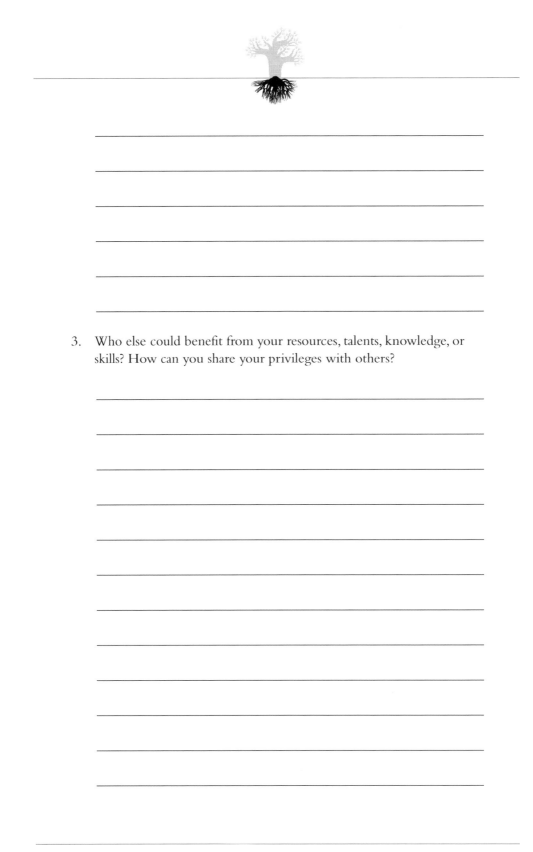

_____

_____

_____

_____

_____

_____

_____

3. Who else could benefit from your resources, talents, knowledge, or
    skills? How can you share your privileges with others?

_____

_____

_____

_____

_____

_____

_____

_____

_____

_____

_____

GOOD THINGS
for Your Spirit

CHAPTER 10

ACT YOUR WAY TO A
NEW WAY OF THINKING

"Keep your thoughts positive because your thoughts become your words. Keep your words positive because your words become your behaviors. Keep your behaviors positive because your behaviors become your habits. Keep your habits positive because your habits become your values. Keep your values positive because your values become your destiny."

MAHATMA GANDHI

Old habits die hard, and it's tough to get new habits to stick.

Years ago, one of my spiritual leaders used this phrase, and it really stuck with me:

"It's easier to act your way to a new way of thinking than to think your way to a new way of acting."

He had to repeat the sentence twice before I fully comprehended what he was saying. It's okay. Read it again. Three or four times, maybe.

"It's easier to act your way into a new way of thinking than to think your way to a new way of acting."

We have good intentions. Eat better. Exercise more. Go back to school. Remember birthdays.

But life gets in the way of even the brightest ideas. Good intentions get swept aside by today's whirlwind of problems and opportunities.

Without action, thoughts are just thoughts that don't result in a sustainable change in behavior.

So when you think of a personal change you want to make, turn it into action. Identify at least one specific thing you will do to change your behavior. And then do it! Pass up the candy bar and eat a banana this afternoon. Join a gym and take the complimentary orientation to meet the trainer and learn to use the equipment. Apply to graduate school. Set your calendar with reminders for the next three months' birthdays.

Act once. Then act again. Gather momentum. You'll increase your odds of sustaining that change in your behavior.

GOOD QUESTIONS

1. What gets in the way when you need to take action? Time? People?
    Job? Something else? What's that about?

    _____

    _____

    _____

    _____

    _____

    _____

    _____

    _____

    _____

    _____

2. What is one thing you've been thinking of doing differently? What is
    one action you can take to make that happen?

    _____

    _____

    _____

    _____

    _____

_____

_____

_____

_____

_____

_____

_____

_____

3. Who can hold you accountable for taking that action?

_____

_____

_____

_____

_____

_____

_____

_____

_____

_____

_____

_____

GOOD THINGS
for Your Spirit

CHAPTER 11

YOUR WORDS AND ACTIONS IMPACT THE WORDS AND ACTIONS OF OTHERS

Life Lesson
by Laura Hornell Yudys

In elementary school, one of my assignments was to interview my parents about marriage. While I don't remember the specifics of the interview, the individual questions, or even what grade I got on the assignment, I do remember my mom's take-home message:

One of the keys to a happy and healthy marriage is that "actions speak louder than words."

At the time, I had to ask her to explain what she meant. To be honest, I don't think I really understood even after her explanation. But that moment and message stuck with me, and as I've gotten older I have begun to understand what Mom was saying.

Now I realize that this message rings true not only in my marriage but in all aspects of my life. I've heard Mom's voice when making time to get together with college friends who no longer live nearby, when volunteering for a committee at work that I feel strongly about, even when deciding to spend a Saturday volunteering instead of channel surfing on the couch.

Of the many things Mom has taught me, the lesson that it takes more than just words to show you care has been one of the most meaningful—even if it did take time for me to understand.

It's the day after Christmas. People flock to retailers to return merchandise or take advantage of sales. Parking lots are jammed. Store aisles are crowded. Products are out of stock or out of place. Piles of returned items clutter the checkout areas. Lines are long. Both customers and clerks are edgy and exhausted from the holiday bustle.

As a young college student, I experienced this tension at the cash register while working at a department store during holiday break. One episode stands out:

> A woman approached and threw a box on the counter. "I got this as a gift and want to return it," she said briskly.

> "Of course," I said. "Do you have the receipt?" She did not. I explained that without a receipt, I could give her store credit, pointing to the policy outlined on a laminated card next to the register.

> "I don't need store credit, because I don't even shop here!" she said in a huff. "I'll take cash."

> Everyone nearby heard as she continued to rant about policies, crowds, and her unfinished to-do list.

> At that point, I felt someone step into my register area. The store manager, a polished woman with a commanding presence, addressed the customer with a firm voice, "Ma'am, our store policy has always been to provide store credit when customers do not have a receipt. Deb has conducted herself professionally, according to our policy. I expect you to treat her and our other employees with the respect they show to you. If you can do that, we are happy to help you; if not, you can shop elsewhere."

> The woman immediately calmed down, apologized to me and accepted the store credit.

I have never forgotten that store manager's example of leadership. What grace! When I'm the customer in a challenging retail or service situation, my memory of her prompts me to treat the other person with respect. More often than not, choosing respect results in a positive outcome.

Have you ever been in one of the following situations?

- You approach the gate attendant about a delayed or cancelled flight.
- You call your utility provider about a discrepancy on your bill.
- You meet with a school counselor or principal to discuss a situation with your child.

How did you enter that conversation? What was the result?

Every action has a reaction. Your actions affect how others will respond to you. Your tone—whether spoken or written or even in body language—influences how others will interpret your message. So before you speak or act, ask yourself, "What am I bringing to this conversation, and how can I get this person to hear me and work with me?"

GOOD QUESTIONS

1. Think about a recent conversation that did not go well. What part did you play in that result? What words did you use that may have triggered the other person's emotion? What actions did you take that may have caused a negative reaction in them?

_____

_____

_____

_____

_____

_____

_____

2. How could you have prepared yourself to enter that interaction differently? What could you have said or done to conduct yourself with grace and be respectful to the other person?

_____

_____

_____

_____

_____

_____

_____

3. Think about an upcoming conversation that may be tough. How can you prepare so your words and actions affect the other person in a positive way?

_____

_____

_____

_____

_____

_____

_____

GOOD THINGS
for Your Spirit

CHAPTER 12

SOMEONE NEEDS TO BE THE BIG PERSON, HOW ABOUT YOU?

What's in your heart?
by Doug Andresen

We once had a group leader at work who treated everyone poorly, including me. One day, I'd had enough of being disrespected. I walked up to him and said, "Why are you always treating me like crap? I don't do that to you."

Taken aback, he stopped talking, and never treated me that way again. Instead of getting caught up in his game, I wanted to do what was right for me and others—to be the big person, like my mom always said.

Since then, if people are saying negative things to or about me, I don't feed into it. I walk away or work hard to prove them wrong. I won't let anyone have power over me.

Whatever is in your heart comes out of your mouth. If your heart is dark, driven by anger, unhappiness, or sadness, it can swallow you up. If your heart is light, filled with harmony and happiness, you'll express that light in your soul. That's what I want—to be happy, because negativity bums me out!

I wish I had a dollar for every time I heard my mother say:

"Someone needs to be the big person, how about you?"

Whenever I hear someone complaining about another person (and sometimes it's me), this phrase rings through my head. I've even been known to say it to my brothers and to my children. Maybe it's true that we become more and more like our parents …

But I digress.

Being the big person may not make you filthy rich. It does open you to greater richness in your relationships. Countless times, I have wanted to walk away from or dismiss someone to avoid getting involved in drama or because I didn't want them to have the upper hand. But then my mother's words pass through my head: "Someone needs to be the big person. How about you?" And I think, "Yeah, how about me?"

Being the big person means letting go of your need to win or to be in control. It means humbling yourself, having a tough conversation, and reaching out to connect with another person or heal a fractured relationship.

Being the big person means doing the right thing for all. It means tearing down your own defensiveness, competitiveness, and insecurity—the things that wall you off from others.

I never regret the choice to step up in this way. More often than not, I end up with a new appreciation for the other person, a healthy dose of learning for myself, and a more honest relationship for both of us.

GOOD QUESTIONS

1. Do you have a relationship that is broken or tense? What has created the fracture? What have you done to contribute to the problem?

    _____

    _____

    _____

    _____

    _____

    _____

    _____

    _____

    _____

    _____

2. What kind of relationship do you want with the other person? How can you change your behavior to make that happen?

    _____

    _____

    _____

    _____

    _____

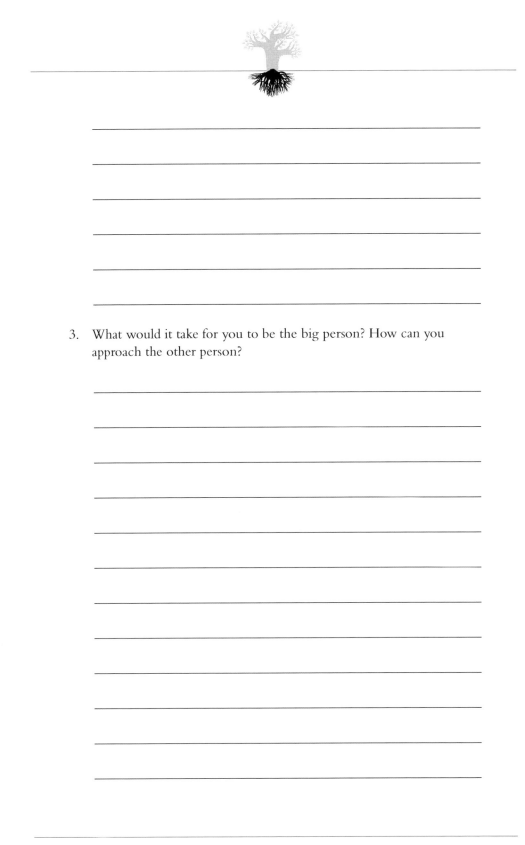

_____

_____

_____

_____

_____

3. What would it take for you to be the big person? How can you approach the other person?

_____

_____

_____

_____

_____

_____

_____

_____

_____

_____

GOOD THINGS
for Your Spirit

CHAPTER 13

CHOICES BEGET CHOICES

My husband and I began dating during our senior year of high school. Pretty quickly, we knew we wanted to spend our lives together. We discussed the kind of life we wanted to lead, deciding to delay marriage and children in order to create that life. We made each choice—where to live, when and where to go to school, when and how many children to have—with careful consideration for our shared vision of that future life.

That's not to say we were rigid. Even though we knew what we wanted, we stayed flexible and open to new experiences. Sometimes, one choice opens an unexpected door to another choice. As we have navigated decisions together—even now as we settle into an empty nest—we have used our common goals and values as a guide.

Choices beget choices. Think about each of these choices and the future choices they might create:

- Go to college, delay college, or don't go to college
- Accept a job or turn it down
- Marry young, marry later in life, or never marry
- Move to a new city or settle in the town where you grew up
- Buy a home or rent a home
- Have children or don't have children

Decisions like these can have long-term consequences. So even those of us with strong instincts need to set impulses aside and do some analysis. We have to step back and ask, "How will this choice affect my life in the future? Is it consistent with my priorities and values? Will it move me toward the full life I want to create?"

GOOD QUESTIONS

1. Consider a major choice you've made in the last five to ten years.
    How has that decision affected how you live now? How has it created
    additional choices you now face?

    _____

    _____

    _____

    _____

    _____

    _____

    _____

    _____

    _____

2. Think about a choice you face right now. What options do you have?
    What is the impact of each option in the short term and in the
    future?

    _____

    _____

    _____

    _____

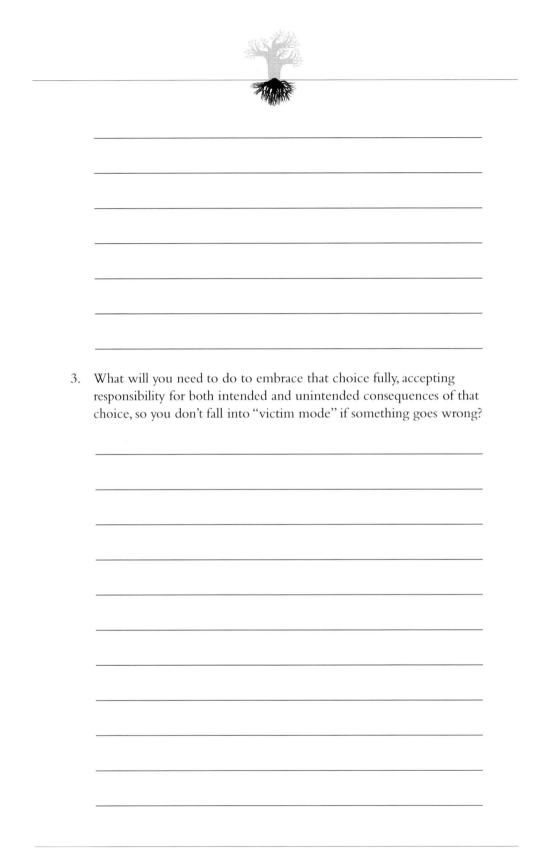

_____

_____

_____

_____

_____

_____

_____

_____

3. What will you need to do to embrace that choice fully, accepting responsibility for both intended and unintended consequences of that choice, so you don't fall into "victim mode" if something goes wrong?

_____

_____

_____

_____

_____

_____

_____

_____

_____

_____

_____

GOOD THINGS
for Your Spirit

CHAPTER 14

NO REGRETS

---

*"Accept everything about yourself—I mean everything.
You are you, and that is the beginning and the end—
no apologies, no regrets."*

CLARK MOUSTAKAS

When my husband finished graduate school, he had several job offers in different parts of the country, but none in Boston, where we were living at the time. In our two years there, I had fallen in love with New England and all that it offered—the sense of history, a job I loved, the proximity to the ocean and fresh, affordable seafood.

Bill knew relocating was a lot to ask of me, so as he prepared to pursue work in another market, he let me choose our next home city. Even though he gave me this choice, and even after we moved to my chosen city of Chicago, I was frustrated and resentful. I dug myself into a "regret rut" for many months, unable to let go of my dream of living the rest of my life in Boston.

My mind finally shifted when my mother-in-law, who had patiently listened to me complain for several weeks, asked me this question:

> *"Are you at the point yet where you can look at this as an opportunity?"*

"Heck, no!" was my gut response. But her question forced me to start thinking of how I could make the most of the situation, rather than pining for my old life in Boston.

Once I relinquished those hard feelings, I noticed that our move to Chicago had created unforeseen "good things." My career blossomed and took me to places I wouldn't have thought possible. Our children enjoyed close relationships with extended family within driving distance. My oldest daughter met her husband at a local business. I've served on four wonderful not-for-profit boards. I developed an active network of friends and colleagues in my neighborhood and all over the country.

I have not always been happy about the twists and turns in my life's pathway, but those experiences have created the person I am today. Everything I am now is because of the life I've led.

> *Everything you are today is because of the life you've led.*

Harboring regrets anchors you in the past and keeps you from being fully engaged in the life that is right in front of you. When you're inclined to say "if only" or "I should have," stop and look for good things. Chances are, the "misfortune" you are tempted to regret has actually given you unexpected lessons, connections, or wisdom.

GOOD QUESTIONS

1. Name one thing you have regretted in your life. Why do you regret it? How has that regret prevented you from moving on to new things?

_____

_____

_____

_____

_____

_____

_____

_____

2. What did you learn about yourself from that experience, and how has it shaped the person you've become? How can you reframe that regret as a "good thing?"

_____

_____

_____

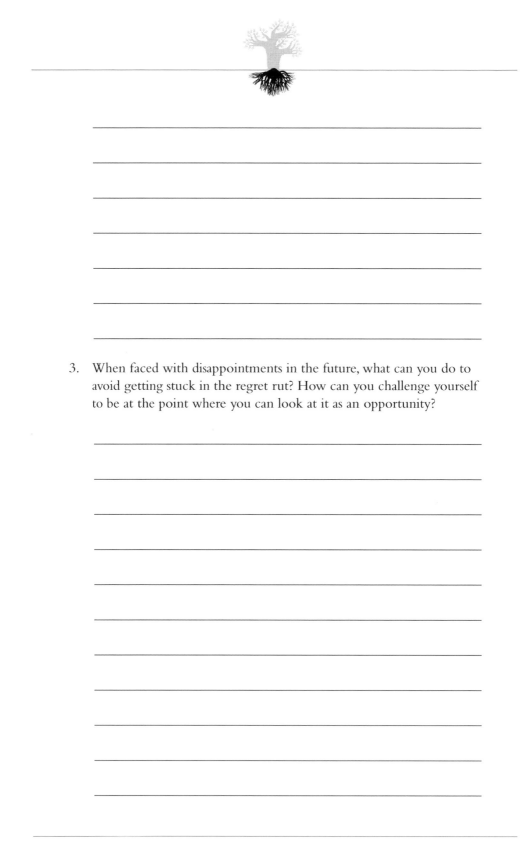

_____

_____

_____

_____

_____

_____

_____

3. When faced with disappointments in the future, what can you do to avoid getting stuck in the regret rut? How can you challenge yourself to be at the point where you can look at it as an opportunity?

_____

_____

_____

_____

_____

_____

_____

_____

_____

_____

_____

SECTION TWO

GOOD THINGS
for Your Personal Life

The chapters in this section are designed to inspire you to get the most out of your Personal life—to appreciate the sequencing of your full life and your relationships with family and friends, and to enhance your engagement with the world around you.

GOOD THINGS
for Your Personal Life

CHAPTER 15

YOUR LIFE AS A CHAPTER BOOK

Song Titles
by Bud Hornell

Man by nature is not a solitary animal. While more people may be adapting to the single way of life each day, "Me and My Shadow" is not an operative lifestyle for me.

As a child, I learned certain principles from my parents; in the military, I was introduced to discipline in large-scale organizations; in my work, I accepted accountability and responsibility; in my marriage, I learned caring and compromise; as a parent, I learned to put others ahead of myself; in my setbacks, I learned resiliency; and now in retirement, I hope to find fulfillment and new avenues never before traveled.

Interaction with others permeates each chapter in our lives. We are—or, more correctly, should be—motivated by others to find new values, new disciplines, and new modes of behavior.

Think about initiating an entirely new, unfamiliar chapter in your life. Set a goal. Volunteer. If possible, take a cruise or travel. Find someone or something that needs you, something that will make you feel good about yourself. If you suddenly find yourself alone, look around and reach out. You may find someone in similar circumstances. Who knows what may happen?

Think positive. If you are lucky—and willing to risk it—you may find that love can be good "The Second Time Around." It won't be easy. Old habits die hard, and you may need to make compromises you never had to make before. But "That's Life." If you're willing to try, you could be amazed at the enjoyment and rewards that lie ahead.

T hings change as we get older. Each decade brings experiences, wisdom, challenges, and opportunities for growth.

When my children were young, I invested a great deal of time and energy in them, trading off volunteer activities and graduate school. Once they were older and more independent, I was able to invest more of myself in other activities. During their teenage years, when they needed to assert their independence, I was glad to have a "full life," because I didn't define myself as just their mother.

My sense of identity and satisfaction came from multiple sources: work, family, friends, and not-for-profit work, to name a few. Because I had other areas of focus, I was able to navigate those teenage years with more objectivity, which served us all well. I was able to view that time as just one of the chapters of our life together, knowing there would be many more to come—that this wasn't the end. I kept things in perspective.

My children tell me now that I set an example of what their lives could be: a mix of work, family, and volunteer activities, all of which are important. They have begun to approach their own lives as a series of chapters full of good things.

So, begin to think of your life in five-year chapters. What you need in your full life at age twenty-five may be very different than what you need at thirty-five or forty or fifty-five. As you near the start of each new chapter, take time to realign your priorities so you are ready to turn the page.

GOOD QUESTIONS

1. What chapter of life are you in right now? What parts of your full life are your top priorities in this chapter?

_____

_____

_____

_____

_____

_____

_____

_____

_____

_____

_____

2. What activities and people require more of your attention now? Which can take a back seat?

_____

_____

_____

_____

_____

_____

_____

_____

_____

_____

_____

3. What will you do to navigate this chapter with objectivity and
    perspective?

_____

_____

_____

_____

_____

_____

_____

_____

_____

_____

_____

GOOD THINGS
for Your Personal Life

CHAPTER 16

NO LIMITS

While swimming laps one morning, I noticed the woman in the lane next to me was an amazing swimmer—fast and graceful, with beautiful form. What I didn't realize, at first, was that she was blind. Just imagine swimming thirty laps without being able to see where you're going.

Since then, whenever I feel limited or don't have the resources or courage to do something, I think of that woman, swimming lap after lap without fear or hesitation.

We all face obstacles to achieving a full life. Instead of complaining or making excuses, figure out how to make things happen for you. Rather than creating artificial limits, visualize yourself confidently achieving your goals.

And if you ever doubt yourself, remember the blind swimmer—fast and graceful, with beautiful form.

GOOD QUESTIONS

1. What limits do you put on yourself? Why?

_____

_____

_____

_____

_____

_____

_____

_____

_____

_____

_____

2. If you didn't have limits, what could you achieve?

_____

_____

_____

_____

_____

_____

_____

_____

_____

_____

_____

_____

3. How can you be more like the blind swimmer, approaching life
    without fear or hesitation?

_____

_____

_____

_____

_____

_____

_____

_____

_____

_____

_____

EMBRACE DECADE TRANSITIONS

Reflecting on the Decades
by John Weaver

With each passing decade in my life, there have been significant events marking time's progression. In one decade alone, from ages twenty-two to thirty-two, I experienced at least one major life event each year—college graduation, new job, geographic relocation, marriage, home purchase, birth of a child.

The pace of change didn't slow as I built a career and raised a family through my thirties and forties. But the decade transition points never felt all that significant. It was all part of seemingly never-ending, continuous advancement.

However, as I approached the end of my forties and began the transition into my fifties, there seemed to be simultaneous signs of rewarding stability and fundamental instability across the key aspects of my life. On the one hand, my wife and I were celebrating twenty-five years of marriage, and our three children had left home and successfully launched into adulthood. On the other hand, I found myself working at a company that seemed misaligned with my core values regarding growth, quality of work, and personal respect for individuals.

Finally recognizing the need to manage a different type of transition, I chose to leverage the skills I had built over the preceding decades. I entered a new profession and ultimately became a Managing Partner in a firm where fundamental values are a core part of our operating model. So, by embracing the transition into my fifties, I have a renewed sense for what's most important professionally and am able to more fully appreciate the joys of personal success.

Bring on the next decade!

Years ago, I heard of a concept called the "thirties transition," which suggests that between the ages of twenty-eight and thirty-two, people experience a significant transition. During this time, they make major life changes such as marriage, divorce, having children, having affairs, buying a home, and returning to school.

With friends and clients, I've observed similar transitions occurring not just between the twenties and thirties, but at each decade. Some of these transitions are easier than others, but all require some kind of adjustment period. These shifts manifest in different ways, but are usually marked by a period of questioning, uneasiness, and frustration. Those who are unaware of or fight the transition may act out, suffer from depression, or make risky choices. Those who embrace the transition period as a time of self-reflection and preparing for what's next are able to ease their way into the next decade and welcome the opportunities ahead of them.

GOOD QUESTIONS

1. How have you learned and grown in the last decade?

2. What hopes and concerns do you have for the next decade, with regard to family, friends, work, finances, health, etc.?

_____

_____

_____

_____

_____

_____

3.   What's next for you? How will you define the next decade?

_____

_____

_____

_____

_____

_____

_____

_____

_____

BE A LIFE-LONG LEARNER

Mom, daughter receiving degrees from Benedictine
by Christopher Placek, for the "Daily Herald" newspaper

As Laura Hornell waited to accept her undergraduate degree from the University of Illinois in 2009, she heard names being called of graduates who were from the same family.

About 10 years before, her mom, Deb, had stopped taking graduate classes at Benedictine University in Lisle as she focused on running her own business and raising three children in Glen Ellyn.

Laura Hornell, about to enter Benedictine's nutrition and wellness master's program, had a vision. "I just thought, 'That could be me and my mom up there,'" she said. "I told her, 'I want you to go back to school and finish your master's and I want us to walk together.'"

Two years later, that vision will become reality. The Hornells will join about 1,000 other students who will receive degrees May 15 during Benedictine's 118th commencement convocation.

To read the rest of this article, published in the "Daily Herald" on May 15, 2011, visit:
http://www.dailyherald.com/article/20110515/news/705159930/

Going to college was an important goal I set for myself at a young age, and something my dad expected of me as well. So I became the first person in my family to earn a college degree. Having that degree opened up the world to me, and I've been a proponent of higher education ever since. In fact, my children would tell you that college was "non-negotiable."

Throughout my adult life, I've sought additional learning experiences: taking on challenging assignments at work, getting involved in not-for-profit work, starting piano lessons in my mid-fifties, and achieving certification as a Master Gardener.

The ultimate test for this life-long learner was when my daughter Laura challenged me to return to graduate school. The day she received her bachelor's degree, she declared that she wanted me to walk with her when she received her master's degree from the local university where I had started my own graduate studies several years earlier. Holding fast to a vision of the two of us together in cap and gown, I completed 44 credit hours in less than two years—and we did walk together on commencement day. Not only was it an honor to celebrate that day with my daughter, it was one of the crowning achievements of my life, and I know my dad would have been proud.

Training or education you received ten or twenty years ago does not necessarily prepare you to keep up with the world today, as technology and travel make the world smaller and more accessible. And, as you move through the chapters of life, you may develop new interests or discover pastimes that require you to learn something new.

You're never too old, and it's never too late. Be a life-long learner.

GOOD QUESTIONS

1. What changes have you seen in your field of work or your interests in
   the last five years? What knowledge or skills do you need in order to
   compete—or, better yet, shine?

   _____

   _____

   _____

   _____

   _____

   _____

   _____

   _____

   _____

   _____

2. What have you been interested in learning more about, but haven't
   made time to do so? What would you have to do to pursue that
   learning?

   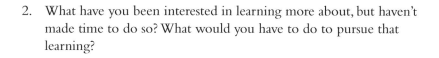

   _____

   _____

   _____

_____

_____

_____

_____

_____

_____

_____

3. Who can hold you accountable for pursuing a learning goal, and
    celebrate with you when you achieve it?

_____

_____

_____

_____

_____

_____

_____

_____

_____

_____

GOOD THINGS
for Your Personal Life

CHAPTER 19

PRACTICE BUCKET MANAGEMENT

The Juggling Act
by Catherine Lanucha

Quality of life and professional fulfillment have been a constant juggling act for me. This struggle resurfaced not long after I bought my first home and my young family settled into our life in the suburbs. On the surface, everything appeared in alignment. Yet all my spare energy was focused on solving a negative job situation instead of nurturing my personal life.

I decided to take a week off to reflect on my career. As it happened, my hiatus coincided with an appearance on a mentoring panel to discuss my personal brand. Frankly, I felt like a fraud speaking to high-potential women when I felt so disoriented.

Before the panel, my dear friend and mentor, Deb, recognized that I was wrestling with some familiar demons. She did not ask what was wrong, but simply asked:

"Catherine, how are your buckets?"

She elaborated that to have a full life I had to allocate my precious resources in key areas: relationships, career, and personal growth. I could have taken several minutes rationalizing the state of my nearly empty buckets. Instead, I chose to be honest. I looked into my buckets and admitted they were not a true reflection of me. I decided to take some time to reflect on what was important, realign my priorities, and make sure the state of my buckets matched those priorities.

Since then, when I feel tempted to juggle, I focus on my buckets instead.

As a gardener, I'm always hauling various buckets around the yard, filled with mulch, compost, or potting soil. Because I want to be efficient, I practice good "bucket management." I make sure the buckets contain just the right amount of material for the job. I prevent spills by not overfilling buckets. I don't leave empty buckets lying around.

It strikes me that we need to practice good "bucket management" as we tend our full lives as well.

Imagine a group of buckets, each representing a necessary part of your life: work, family, friends, hobbies, and whatever else you consider a priority. Picture the buckets as full, partially full, or empty—reflecting how you feel about that part of your life.

When you feel like your life is out of balance or you feel stressed, think about those buckets. Are some spilling over, while others are empty?

During the various chapters of your life, not all buckets need to be equally full. But you probably don't want any empties, and you may not be able to manage a bucket that's overflowing. So if any of your containers are approaching or have reached these stages, consider what you need to do to restore your buckets to appropriate levels.

GOOD QUESTIONS

1. What do your buckets look like? Which are too empty or too full?

    _____

    _____

    _____

    _____

    _____

    _____

    _____

    _____

2. In this chapter of your full life, where should the bucket levels be to create satisfaction for you? Where should you be investing time and energy?

    _____

    _____

    _____

    _____

    _____

    _____

    _____

3. What choices are you making that are creating the bucket levels? What do you need to do to maintain or change various levels?

_____

_____

_____

_____

_____

_____

_____

_____

_____

4. What actions will you take to practice good bucket management?

_____

_____

_____

_____

_____

_____

_____

_____

GOOD THINGS
for Your Personal Life

CHAPTER 20

TURN OFF TECHNOLOGY AND TUNE INTO THE WORLD AROUND YOU

What do you see in this picture?
How many different plants do you see?
How many butterflies?
What would it smell like in this garden?
How warm would it be in this scene?
What would it feel like to have a butterfly
brush your cheek with its wing?

When my children were small, one of their favorite games was "I Spy"—a simple race to see who would be first to identify a nearby object with a few basic clues. To play, we had to listen to each other and be observant about what was going on around us.

Now, when I see a parent talking on the phone while pushing a baby stroller, I spy a missed opportunity for parent and child to explore how buds turn into leaves, how mother birds feed their babies, how worms come out after the rain. When I see two people sitting at a restaurant focused on their smart phones instead of each other, I spy a lost moment for them to engage in meaningful conversation.

Technology lets us connect and interact with ease, increasing our points of contact and giving us access to a wide world of information. This is a good thing. But one downside of our highly technical world is that we may miss out on fully experiencing the world around us. Engrossed in gadgets and information, we become reactive, responding only to what is in front of us. When was the last time you stopped, took a wide look around, noticed, and reflected on something from the natural world around you?

Sure, technology allows us to communicate and connect with others—but generally in a one-sided, reactive way. Texting, for example, conveys only a one-dimensional message (maybe a bit more if you use emoticons ☺). What is lost is full, three-dimensional conversation: the give-and-take; the pacing between two people; the time to really hear a message and comprehend the emotion behind it; the patience to reflect on how to respond so the other person understands you; the thoughtfulness to ask, "How would I like to receive this message?"

Here are some radical ideas to tune into the world around you:

- Declare meals a technology-free zone: no TV, phones, radios, headphones, or ear buds allowed. Talk with your tablemates. If you're dining alone in a restaurant, observe others or strike up a conversation with the server.
- Leave your phone or audio player at home and take a walk. Go alone or take a dog, friend, family member, or child. Use your senses to experience the world. What do you see, feel, smell, and hear around you?

- Read a book without any "noise" distracting you.
- Establish time for reflection by turning off technology for 30 minutes—maybe as part of your morning routine, during your commute to or from work, or at the end of the day.

GOOD QUESTIONS

1. What is one step you can take to turn off technology and tune into the world?

_____

_____

_____

_____

_____

_____

_____

_____

_____

_____

_____

_____

_____

_____

2. What would you gain by doing this? What would you lose?

_____

_____

_____

_____

_____

_____

_____

_____

3. What can you do on a daily basis to fully experience the world
   around you without feeling disconnected or out of touch?

_____

_____

_____

_____

_____

_____

_____

_____

PARENTS: BE CLEAR ON YOUR ROLE AND DON'T LOSE YOURSELF IN THE PROCESS

Moment of Truth
By Nancy Hoying

On a recent "college shopping" trip with my daughter, the high school counselor's voice resonated in my head: "Remember to let your child do the introduction and ask questions on the college campuses. It sends the wrong signal if you do the talking for them."

So there I was, on our very first college visit, and the admissions counselor smiled at me and established eye contact! I had to physically bite my tongue, hold my breath, smile, and turn to my daughter. I'm sure I looked a little strange. But this was a parenting moment of truth for me—to take a backseat and let my daughter do the talking, take initiative, and ask the questions to navigate her own college selection process.

This need to let go and limit (notice I didn't say "stop") my urge to protect, advocate, and make decisions for my child came much earlier than I expected—long before we started shopping for colleges. Children tend to have radar to know best what will work in a situation, and often just need guidance to figure it out. When they introduce a problem to us, perhaps by coming home crying or upset, our instinct is to fix it. But by guiding them through the problem-solving process—asking questions, listening empathetically, and discovering solutions together—we empower the child to take action and become more committed to the outcome. And by figuring things out for themselves, children feel a sense of accomplishment and ownership.

Incidentally, my daughter was one of the only students who asked questions during those college visits. We both found our way.

The sole objective of parenting is to prepare your children to leave you. This is a serious endeavor, not for the faint of heart!

In the beginning, children depend completely on their parents for everything: what to eat, when to sleep, what to wear. But as they mature, children need to separate from their parents in order to be physically and emotionally ready for adulthood.

This was a huge "aha" for me when my children became adolescents. The little people whose daily lives I had overseen from birth didn't need me to do that anymore. In fact, they rebelled when I tried to do too much. Emotionally, this was very hard for me. I had to mourn the loss of that close parent–child relationship before I could be open to a new parent–adult child relationship.

I decided to find ways to fill the "gap" with other activities and interests. I took on challenging consulting projects, joined a not-for-profit board, and played golf with good friends. It was still an adjustment, but those activities made it easier to cope.

It's easy for parents to invest their sense of identity and self-worth in the parenting role. It's also very dangerous. Many parents define themselves and their success by their children's accomplishments—grades, sports, friends—and become competitive with other parents.

If you are a parent, make sure you have other interests in your life. The time will come when your children will leave you. If you've invested all of yourself in them, you will be lost.

GOOD QUESTIONS

1. How do you define your success as a parent?

_____

_____

_____

_____

_____

_____

_____

_____

_____

_____

2. In what ways are you preparing your children for independence?

_____

_____

_____

_____

_____

_____

_____

_____

_____

_____

_____

_____

3. In what ways are you preparing yourself for your children's
   independence?

_____

_____

_____

_____

_____

_____

_____

_____

_____

_____

_____

GOOD THINGS

for Your Personal Life

MEALTIME IS AN OPPORTUNITY TO NOURISH YOUR BODY AND YOUR RELATIONSHIPS

Family dinner August 2009

Birthday dinner September 2012

When I was a child, my family sat down together for breakfast and dinner every day until, as teenagers, our jobs and extracurricular activities found us rarely in the same place at the same time. At that point, our family became disconnected, and outside activities took priority over family mealtime.

I vowed that when I had my own family, dinnertime would be sacred. From day one of my marriage, I established a ritual of family dinnertime. As mentioned in the introduction to this book, as a young boy, my son Matt challenged our family to discuss "good things" each night at the table as part of our coming together. Each person had to report out on one or two good things that had happened that day. Our mealtime ritual had become as important to Matt and the rest of our family as it was to me. To this day, when my children come home to visit, we schedule and look forward to "family dinner."

Although many countries still emphasize relaxed dining and conversation at mealtime, the U.S. seems to be moving away from this sentiment. Ever-growing options for fast food and extracurricular activities have challenged the importance of communal mealtime. Even when they are sitting at the same table, many families are focused on the television instead of each other. They are losing the ability to learn about and support each other through conversation.

Choosing to commune with others several times a week allows for a pause in your day, to make or renew connections with others. Try it. Schedule breakfast, lunch, or dinner with a friend or family member(s). It doesn't matter if you meet in a restaurant or at someone's home. Your stomach and your spirit will thank you.

GOOD QUESTIONS

1. When was the last time you ate lunch or dinner with a friend or
    family member, without watching television or checking your phone?

    _____

    _____

    _____

    _____

    _____

    _____

    _____

    _____

    _____

    _____

    _____

2. What would you gain by spending time with others in conversation
    over a meal?

    _____

    _____

    _____

    _____

_____

_____

_____

_____

_____

_____

_____

_____

_____

3. What can you do to nourish your body and relationships? How often will you commit to a meal with others?

_____

_____

_____

_____

_____

_____

_____

_____

_____

GOOD THINGS
for Your Personal Life

CHAPTER 23

BE TRUE TO YOURSELF AND OTHERS

Your Soul is Showing
by Brenda Knapp

For me, the idea of being true to yourself and others is aligned with the popular concept of authentic leadership. In her book, "Simple Abundance," Sarah Ban Breathnack wrote: "The authentic self is the soul made visible."

To be an authentic leader, you have to be an authentic person—honest and real.

It has taken me some time and maturity to be absolutely comfortable with showing my authenticity. I spent many years toning down some of the personality traits that make me uniquely "me," in an effort to fit in (sounds pathetically like junior high school, doesn't it?).

Authenticity comes when we put ourselves out there, embracing our lack of perfection but honoring our excellence and owning our unique strengths. Authentic leaders show up consistently in all interactions, both personal and professional.

Now, one of the greatest compliments someone can give me is, "You are exactly the same person, regardless of the situation." That's not to say that I don't have a different style or tone in the boardroom than I do on the sidelines at a high school soccer game. But my core values and legacy are the same, and they are integrated into how I behave, regardless of the situation. We have to know our overriding values and demonstrate them daily.

Don't be afraid let your soul show. That's authentic!

One of my favorite definitions of success is from the book *Fierce Conversations* by Susan Scott:

"I am successful to the degree that who I am and what I live are in alignment."

This statement speaks to authenticity—being true to your values, and acting in ways that are congruent with the legacy you hope to leave. Other people respond to that authenticity, and trust you because they know they can count on you.

Because integrity is one of my top values, I want others to experience me as a person of integrity. To do that, I strive to keep my word, keep my commitments, and be honest with myself and others about my intentions. My family, friends, and colleagues have come to expect nothing less from me. They deserve nothing less.

If you're true to yourself, you don't compromise your beliefs and values. You're also honest about your intentions—what you really want from situations and from other people. You don't play games or act on assumptions, and you have a lot more fun and a lot less drama in your life.

GOOD QUESTIONS

1. In what ways are you true to your legacy and values? How can you be sure you continue on this path?

_____

_____

_____

_____

_____

_____

_____

_____

_____

2. In what ways do you sabotage your legacy and values? What can you do to turn that around?

_____

_____

_____

_____

_____

_____

_____

_____

_____

_____

_____

3. How honest are you about your intentions, with yourself and others? How can you represent your intentions more honestly?

_____

_____

_____

_____

_____

_____

_____

_____

_____

_____

GOOD THINGS
for Your Personal Life

CHAPTER 24

YOU CAN DO ANYTHING YOU PUT YOUR MIND TO

Fanning the Flames
by Bruce Andresen

My sister Deb is one of my mentors. From an early age, she knew what she wanted and worked on a plan to get there. Our mom would tell us, "You can be anything you want to be." Mom instilled in us the need to set goals and plan how to reach them. She also said, "Don't let anyone steal your dream."

My involvement in the martial arts has confirmed the need for setting goals, developing a plan, and diligently working that plan. Earning a black belt requires dedication and hard work. My role as instructor is to nurture the small spark of interest in a beginning student and build it into a bonfire that will roar past all obstacles on the road to black belt.

We have a clearly defined curriculum that leads students, step by step, toward that goal. They are rewarded with symbols of their progress, helping them stay motivated and move forward.

The same can be applied to any goal. Set your goal, and then break it up into mini goals. Reward yourself as you reach each step along the way. Fan your internal flame!

Y ou've probably heard this statement before:

You can do anything you put your mind to.

My parents used to say that to me all the time. As a kid, I thought it was a ploy to get me to try new things.

As I got older, I realized my parents were actually talking about attitude. With true conviction, you can make something happen. We weren't unrealistic; I wasn't going to be a professional basketball player or President of the United States. But with clarity about my strengths and goals, I could put together a plan that would make my goals a reality.

My older brother once remarked that what he most admired about me was that I always knew what I wanted and was able to make it happen. He believed my can-do attitude and determination helped me reach my goals. I guess maybe my parents were right.

People often find excuses for not taking action on their wishes or dreams. "I don't have any money." "I don't have time." "I don't know how to get started." There will always be obstacles to accomplishing things that matter. An attitude shift—"If I really want this, I can make it happen"— can be the first step on the path to success.

> *"Could we change our attitude, we should not only see life differently, but life itself would come to be different. Life would undergo a change of appearance because we ourselves had undergone a change of attitude."*
>
> KATHERINE MANSFIELD

GOOD QUESTIONS

1. What is something you've always wanted to do, but didn't know how to get started? What's holding you back?

   _____

   _____

   _____

   _____

   _____

   _____

   _____

   _____

   _____

   _____

2. Envision yourself successfully completing your goal. What would that look like? Who would you have to be to ensure that success?

   _____

   _____

   _____

   _____

_____

_____

_____

_____

_____

_____

_____

3. What are two or three steps you can take to move toward your goal?
    Whose help do you need, and how can you ask for it?

_____

_____

_____

_____

_____

_____

_____

_____

_____

_____

_____

GOOD THINGS
for Your Personal Life

CHAPTER 25

THE POWER OF COMMITMENT

Deb and Bill in 1977 and 2012

My role models for the power of commitment are my parents and in-laws, my maternal grandparents, and my husband's maternal grandparents. All four couples married in their early twenties and remained married until one of the partners died. Each couple faced their share of struggles, but each individual turned to their partner for support to weather those rough patches. They demonstrated that making a choice to be in a relationship with another person requires honesty, courage, and ongoing effort.

Relationships are not always easy, whether with a spouse or partner, siblings, children, or close friends. There are definitely ups and downs—times when you may not like each other much, and other times when you feel a renewed sense of togetherness. As you grow older and wiser, you can begin to let go of the need to control everything, accepting the other person without feeling the need to change them.

There is a tremendous sense of freedom and empowerment that comes from time and experience together.

What works in a healthy, committed relationship? Common values and goals; the belief that you are in this together; respect and caring for the other person; and making a conscious decision to work things out when times get tough. True commitment is worth it in the long run.

GOOD QUESTIONS

1. Who are your role models for the power of commitment? What is it
    about them that you admire?

    _____

    _____

    _____

    _____

    _____

    _____

    _____

    _____

    _____

    _____

2. Think about a relationship you have in which you want a strong
    commitment. What would you need to do to truly commit to that
    relationship? What would you gain? What would you have to let go?

    _____

    _____

    _____

    _____

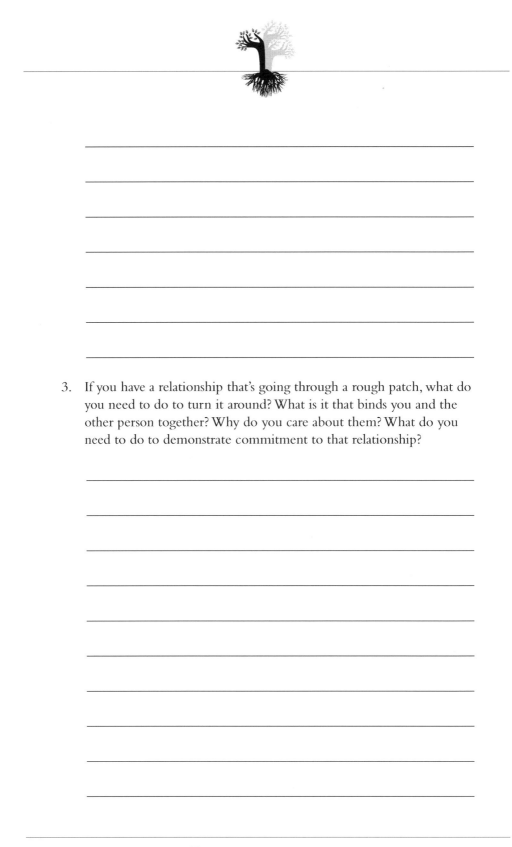

_____

_____

_____

_____

_____

_____

3. If you have a relationship that's going through a rough patch, what do you need to do to turn it around? What is it that binds you and the other person together? Why do you care about them? What do you need to do to demonstrate commitment to that relationship?

_____

_____

_____

_____

_____

_____

_____

_____

SECTION THREE

GOOD THINGS
for Your Professional Life

These chapters speak to you at work—how to add
value, deliver results, develop strong working
relationships, and achieve greater satisfaction.

KNOW WHAT YOU BRING
TO THE TABLE

"If you don't know what you bring to the table, you don't get a seat there."

DAN SCHAWBEL

While in our mid-twenties, my husband and I moved to Boston so he could attend graduate school. Unable to find a teaching position, I had to repackage my experience and skills in order to be considered a viable candidate for jobs in the business world.

The first step was to rethink how teaching skills honed in Louisville, Kentucky would resonate with potential employers more than 800 miles away. I sought out a friend who worked as a banker, and together, we created a resume that spoke the language of business. "Creating lesson plans" became "curriculum development." "Teaching morning and afternoon kindergarten classes" became "creating learning environments for diverse audiences."

The second step was to prepare myself to answer interviewers' tough questions, and to believe I had something of value to offer the business world. I had to put myself in the employer's position and ask myself an important question:

Why should anyone hire you?

So many talented people with so much valuable experience are vying for positions in virtually every field. To land a role, or even just qualify for an interview, you must be able to articulate the value you bring to a particular position.

What knowledge, experience, skills, and perspective do you bring to the table? If you don't know or can't express the answer to this question, you're at a disadvantage. Seek out a friend or career counselor to help you repackage your experience and skills so potential employers hear a solid answer when they ask why they should hire you.

GOOD QUESTIONS

1. What are the top three skills you have that would be of value to an employer?

_____

_____

_____

_____

_____

_____

_____

2. What expertise and knowledge do you have about your chosen field?

_____

_____

_____

_____

_____

_____

_____

3. How have you added value to work or volunteer assignments in the past?

_____

_____

_____

_____

_____

_____

_____

_____

_____

4. How can you position your value to a prospective employer? Finish this statement: "My ability to _____ would make your project successful."

_____

_____

_____

_____

_____

_____

_____

CHAPTER 27

CREATE A YEARLY INDIVIDUAL DEVELOPMENT PLAN (IDP) AND WORK THAT PLAN

Living my Life by Working my Plan
by Judy Oliver Busby

I was one of those people who obsessed over to-do lists. I have even placed things on my list for the sole purpose of crossing them off. Upon reflection, I'm not sure I accomplished more than sustaining my everyday existence.

Then, about eight years ago, I started formally documenting my goals. I began with career goals, and that naturally led to personal goals. And ever since, I've been updating my goals every ninety days. They're categorized this way: Financial & Wealth, Career & Business, Free Time & Fun, Health & Appearance, Personal Development & Learning, and Community & Charity. This process has kept me focused and on track. I opened and now lead a successful consulting business, completed a second master's degree, secured numerous training certifications, exercise regularly, joined two boards, travel frequently, and became a more involved family member and friend.

Helping me stay on course are three accountability partners (Deb is one of them). We meet every quarter to talk about our successes, determine what support we need, and explore the "why" of our efforts. This support, paired with a well-crafted, often-visited list of goals, has helped me achieve even more than I knew I could. Better yet, I've learned a great deal about myself and how I want to live my life.

Companies spend a lot of time creating annual business plans. Many organizations also require employees to create yearly performance plans to align their individual goals and work plans with company strategy.

People who have a plan and work their plan are more focused, more intentional, and much more likely to achieve their goals and feel less stress. Performance development plans can increase employee retention, empowerment, and career advancement.

But how many people take time each year to create a personal development plan? Imagine if you had a personalized roadmap—updated every year—to spell out:

- Your focus or theme for the year
- Actions to accomplish your goal(s)
- Accountability partners who will support your efforts
- Milestones to gauge progress

For the past twenty years, I have established personal goals using this model. Over time, my goals have evolved into a comprehensive Individual Development Plan (IDP) that focuses on the four critical areas of my full life: spiritual, personal, professional, and physical (the same elements used to organize this book). I establish an overarching theme for the year and identify goals for each of the four areas. For each goal, I outline action steps, accountability partners, and milestones.

Creating this yearly IDP keeps me honest.

My accountability partners help me stay true to the plan, too. Accountability partners are the key to successfully reaching your goals. They are the people you identify to provide resources, check in with you on progress, challenge you, and celebrate success. If you know someone is going to ask you about a goal, you will be much more likely to do it. Make sure you are specific about what you need them to do to hold you accountable. Tell them what you need; otherwise, it is a waste of time—yours and theirs.

Having a yearly IDP will keep you honest and keep you on course, too.

GOOD QUESTIONS

1. Do you have a development plan? Why or why not?

    _____

    _____

    _____

    _____

    _____

    _____

    _____

2. What do you want to be different for you? What do you need to do
    to make that happen?

    _____

    _____

    _____

    _____

    _____

    _____

    _____

3. Who will hold you accountable? What do you need them to do?

_____

_____

_____

_____

_____

_____

_____

_____

4. How and when will you assess progress? How will you build in time for reflection and self-correction?

_____

_____

_____

_____

_____

_____

_____

GOOD THINGS
for Your Professional Life

CHAPTER 28

EFFORT = ROI

Return on investment, or "ROI," is a business term that refers to the yield or quantifiable measure of what is achieved from investing money in a business venture.

The principle of ROI can be applied to any endeavor: parenting, gardening, golf, friendships, you name it. With any activity where we invest time or energy or effort, we hope our investment will yield results.

In 2011, my life was full of significant events. We celebrated four graduations: my oldest child and I received our master's degrees, my middle child earned her bachelor's degree, and my youngest graduated from high school. My oldest got married. My youngest left for college. Anticipating the energy and emotion these experiences would demand, I knew I needed to focus my efforts if I had any hope of fully enjoying the year.

So under the theme of "Transition Effort = ROI," I set my annual Individual Development Plan goals to ensure that I invested myself in the right activities. This didn't simplify the schedule; it was still a hectic year. But it was also very joyful and satisfying. I knew where I needed to be and what I needed to do. Maybe even more important, I had a guide for choosing where I didn't need to be and what I didn't need to do.

Some people scurry around trying to be all things to all people, not getting results or satisfaction from their unfocused busy-ness. Putting effort into actions and activities that align with your intended legacy and your Individual Development Plan will result in a satisfying ROI.

With clarity around where to invest effort, you can examine new opportunities with an honest eye: "Is investing effort in this activity going to get me where I need to go?"

GOOD QUESTIONS

1. Where do you need to invest effort or energy to gain greater satisfaction?

    _____

    _____

    _____

    _____

    _____

    _____

    _____

2. Where do you need to stop investing effort and energy? How can you let go of those things?

    _____

    _____

    _____

    _____

    _____

    _____

    _____

3. How will you incorporate ROI-focused goals into your Individual Development Plan (IDP)?

_____

_____

_____

_____

_____

a) Who are your accountability partners for those goals?

_____

_____

_____

_____

_____

b) What will you ask your accountability partners to do to ensure success?

_____

_____

_____

_____

_____

BE MORE CHILDLIKE
AND LESS CHILDISH AT WORK

Kids' Faces
by Bob Sitze

Let's say you want to re-energize the child in you—the kid who most folks instinctively liked back in the day. Here's one way to take a measure of what's still good inside you: How well can people read earnestness in your face? To say that another way, how does your visage still suggest a transparent, truly believable human being prospering under the trappings of adulthood? Does your face still say, "I really, really believe what I'm telling you?"

Most children—especially those too young to be stained by adult expectations or attitudes—are instinctively earnest in what they say. Their facial expressions are an open book, their body language and eyes transparent. When a youngster asks a question, it starts in her or his soul and bursts into the open with a puppy's energy. When a small child converses with you, you're seeing deep inside that brain, without the liability of hypocrisy or manipulation. When a child asks for forgiveness or acceptance, you can see on that child's face the elemental honesty that this humbling moment requires.

Want to be more child-like? Try being earnest, out where the rest of us can see you. Where good things happen.

Far four years after college, I taught kindergarten and nursery school. This was the best possible preparation for navigating corporate America.

Here's why:

Young children are wildly creative. They have an uncanny openness to new ideas. To them, anything is possible. At the same time, they appreciate structure and rules, which enable them to feel safe in exploring the world.

Many adults approach the business world in the exact opposite way. They push against change and innovation. They may act out if they disagree with an idea, if they were not involved, or if they feel put upon. They get defensive and judgmental about ideas or people. They take things personally.

At a time when the global economy is demanding new ways of thinking, we could all learn a lesson from children. We need to be more childlike in how we explore the world around us—looking for opportunities and new ideas. We need to use structures and rules that enable us to feel safe while innovating. We must set our egos aside and see the value in collaborating with others. We need to trust more and fear less so we can embrace change more quickly.

Spend some time with children. And then take what you learned to work.

GOOD QUESTIONS

1. In what situations and with what people are you most receptive to new ideas? Why?

   _____

   _____

   _____

   _____

   _____

   _____

   _____

   _____

   _____

   _____

2. In what situations and with whom do you react with judgment or defensiveness. Why?

   _____

   _____

   _____

   _____

   _____

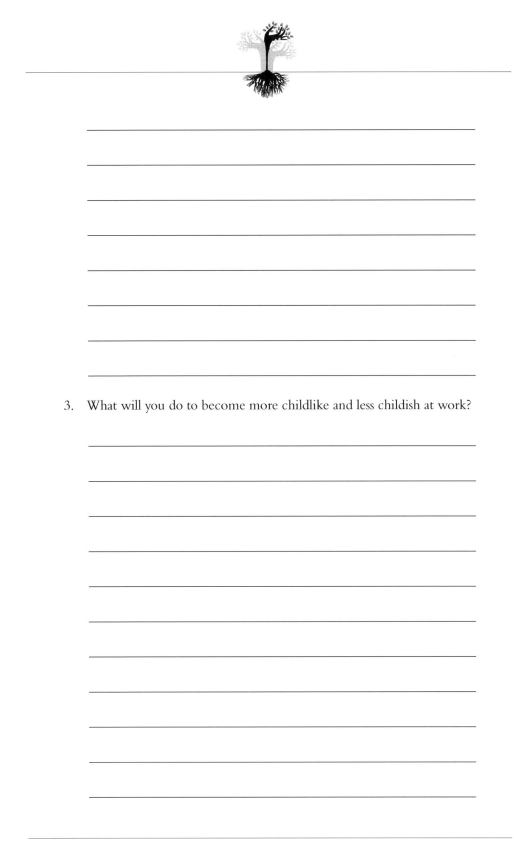

_____

_____

_____

_____

_____

_____

_____

_____

3. What will you do to become more childlike and less childish at work?

_____

_____

_____

_____

_____

_____

_____

_____

_____

_____

_____

_____

CHAPTER 30

BRING SOLUTIONS, NOT EXCUSES

"Whenever you place the cause of one of your actions outside yourself, it's an excuse and not a reason. This rule works for everybody, but it works especially for leaders."

GENERAL COLIN POWELL

Y ou've heard of Murphy's Law: "If something can go wrong, it will."

And things do go wrong. Customers get upset. Products and services don't always get delivered on time or as promised. Employees don't show up for work. People make mistakes.

My team knows that if something goes wrong, I don't want to hear excuses. I want them to identify potential solutions and then determine which one makes the most sense. Excuses waste time and divert energy away from productive results. They create a victim mentality that doesn't settle anything.

When things go wrong, getting into "solution mode" puts you out in front of the situation, where you can resolve a problem more quickly.

You can't possibly anticipate everything that can happen. But looking for solutions, rather than making excuses, can reduce Murphy's power over you.

GOOD QUESTIONS

1. When something goes wrong, how do you respond? Do you begin to think of excuses or do you look for solutions?

_____

_____

_____

_____

_____

_____

_____

_____

_____

_____

2. Think of a time when you did get into "solution mode."
   a) Why were you able to do that?

_____

_____

_____

_____

_____

_____

_____

_____

_____

b) What was the result?

_____

_____

_____

_____

_____

_____

3. What would you need to do to make "solution mode" your routine
    response when something goes wrong?

_____

_____

_____

_____

_____

_____

BE A BAD ASS, NOT A HARD ASS

Deb and her brother Doug on his Harley—two bad asses!

A few years ago, after I was interviewed on a Chicago news show, one of my daughter's twenty-something friends remarked that I was a real "bad ass."

Taken aback, I asked, "What does that mean? A bad ass? Is that a bad thing?"

"Absolutely not," came the reply. "It was a compliment."

This young woman defined "bad ass" as someone who is confident and knows what he or she brings to the table. She saw me presenting myself and my ideas in a way that others respect.

Once I knew the term, I contrasted it with "hard ass"—someone who pushes their way on others, who huffs and puffs, operating from a place of insecurity.

A "hard ass" may get short-term results, but a "bad ass" gets sustainable results and is a lot more fun to work with. Which one sounds better to you?

GOOD QUESTIONS

1. Name at least one bad ass you know. What do you admire about them?

    _____

    _____

    _____

    _____

    _____

    _____

    _____

    _____

2. In what situations are you a bad ass?

    _____

    _____

    _____

    _____

    _____

    _____

    _____

    _____

    _____

3. In what situations are you a hard ass?

_____

_____

_____

_____

_____

_____

_____

_____

_____

_____

4. What would it take for you to live life as a bad ass?

_____

_____

_____

_____

_____

_____

_____

_____

_____

_____

THE ONLY PERSON YOU CAN REALLY MANAGE IS YOURSELF

"The first and best victory is to conquer self."

PLATO

My years as a parent and leader of teams have taught me one big lesson:

I can't make anyone else do anything.

I can establish goals and consequences for behavior, but other individuals will choose whether or not to cooperate. I couldn't make my children get good grades, but I could promote good study habits and set expectations for effort and grades. I can't make employees treat customers with respect, but effective hiring and training can ensure that employees are prepared to serve customers well.

Even though we can't make anyone else do anything, we can do two things: (1) we can manage ourselves, and (2) we can manage our interactions with others.

Primal Leadership, by Daniel Goleman, combines research with practical tips for increasing leadership effectiveness. Goleman describes emotionally intelligent people as exhibiting two tendencies:

- They have personal competence, which means they are self-aware and can manage their emotions.
- They have social competence, which means they are aware of people and situations and can manage relationships.

According to Goleman, "Emotional Intelligence contributes eighty to ninety percent of the competencies that distinguish outstanding from average leaders."

Outstanding leaders know they can't make anyone else do anything. They also know what is within their control: the ability to manage themselves and their interactions with others.

GOOD QUESTIONS

1. In what situations are you trying to make others do something? How is that working?

_____

_____

_____

_____

_____

_____

_____

_____

2. On a scale of one to ten, how would you rate:
   a) Your level of self-awareness of your emotions and how you manage your emotions? Why that rating?

_____

_____

_____

_____

_____

_____

_____

b) Your ability to read cues in others and manage interactions with them? Why that rating?

_____

_____

_____

_____

_____

_____

_____

_____

3. What one or two things can you do differently to manage yourself while interacting with others?

_____

_____

_____

_____

_____

_____

_____

LEADERSHIP IS ABOUT BEHAVIOR, NOT A TITLE

What versus How
by Deana Gelino

I am known for being the one who gets things done, tackling tasks big and small, knocking down barriers (literally, at times) to reach the goal. Most of my career achievement revolved around others telling me, "We have a problem, and we know you can fix it." I can prioritize, lead the heck out of a project, lead the team to complete a task or deliverable, and delegate tasks to the team.

There was a time when I even used that "project" approach with people. Unfortunately, I sometimes treated team members like tasks. Change management and people development were just more "things to do" on my long list.

That's not leadership. And I wanted to be a leader. But until I could truly identify the essence of leadership—what leadership looked and felt like, and what I needed to do to look and feel like a leader—I wasn't able to make the transition.

Once I allowed myself to pause, to reflect, and to focus, I learned a simple and rewarding truth: the "what" may define a project's success, but the more impactful "how" defines leadership.

So now I keep my personal leadership philosophy top of mind. Teams are made up of people, not tasks. I no longer see people management as a project element, but as a leadership responsibility. This has given me entirely new perspective. I am much more self aware, deliberate in my approach, and able to better manage my impact.

Best of all, I now bring to the table a whole new me without giving up "me."

One of my favorite graduate school courses was a class on leadership. While the content was interesting, what fascinated me most was the diverse group of students in the class: a nun from Tanzania, four high school teachers, three first responders, one dietitian, and six business people. And our instructor was a retired military officer who shifted to a second career in business and academia.

We were in education, nutrition, and business. But our conversations were about leaders we had admired in all walks of life. The diversity and intensity of our stories was what educated us about the true meaning of leadership.

So what is leadership? There's a lot of talk about it, and many books on what leadership is, desired traits and skills of leaders, how to "become" a leader, and more.

I don't believe there is one definition or formula for leadership. But every one of the most effective leaders I know acts in these four ways:

1. They know who they are and what they bring to the table.
2. They demonstrate integrity.
3. They treat others with respect.
4. They exhibit courage and are willing to take risks when needed.

Those four sentences describe people and their actions, not job titles. Leaders exist at any level of an organization. People follow them because of who they are, not because of where they sit on an organization chart. Conversely, there are individuals who hold leadership titles, but do not exhibit these traits or inspire others to follow.

True leaders inspire others in whatever role they play.

GOOD QUESTIONS

1. Think of a person you consider a leader. What is it about that person that makes you consider him or her a leader?

   _____

   _____

   _____

   _____

   _____

   _____

   _____

   _____

   _____

   _____

2. How would people describe you? Would they call you a leader? Why or why not?

   _____

   _____

   _____

   _____

   _____

_____

_____

_____

_____

_____

_____

3. Starting today, what can you do to act like a leader: practicing self-awareness, integrity, respect for others, and courage?

_____

_____

_____

_____

_____

_____

_____

_____

_____

_____

_____

CHAPTER 34

IN THE ABSENCE OF AUTHORITY, PEOPLE LOOK FOR LEADERSHIP

"I wanted a perfect ending. Now I've learned, the hard way, that some poems don't rhyme, and some stories don't have a clear beginning, middle, and end. Life is about not knowing, having to change, taking the moment and making the best of it, without knowing what's going to happen next. Delicious Ambiguity."

GILDA RADNER

One of my graduate school classes was a study of human behavior in the absence of structure. The professor offered no syllabus and no agenda. He even declared that he had no role. He simply instructed us to do what we needed to do as a group over the course of two weekends—to be aware of how the group interacted, and to gain self-awareness of how our behavior impacted the rest of the group.

Those two weekends were among the most frustrating times in my career. Without structure or clear roles, we didn't know what to do with ourselves. Ideas to jumpstart the group met with criticism. There was tension, silence, and numerous attacks on style or personality. I kept thinking about the amount of money we had spent to sit in a room with ten strangers who couldn't agree on anything. Sitting there felt like a big waste of time.

But I did learn one significant and valuable lesson:

> *In an ambiguous situation—lacking authority, structure, clear roles, goals, and outcomes—people look for leadership.*

People want someone to show them a path out of ambiguity, to provide direction, insight, or structure so they can make sense of the situation and manage themselves accordingly.

Our complex, global economy is a case study in ambiguity. The rules are unclear about how to be successful, so people flounder.

So, in the absence of authority, there is tremendous opportunity for those who have the courage to step into leadership and make a difference. Someone needs to be the leader. How about you?

GOOD QUESTIONS

1. How comfortable are you with ambiguity? How does that help you or hinder you when faced with new or unclear situations?

_____

_____

_____

_____

_____

_____

_____

_____

_____

_____

_____

2. Where do you see an opportunity to demonstrate leadership by providing ideas, structure, or clarity?

_____

_____

_____

_____

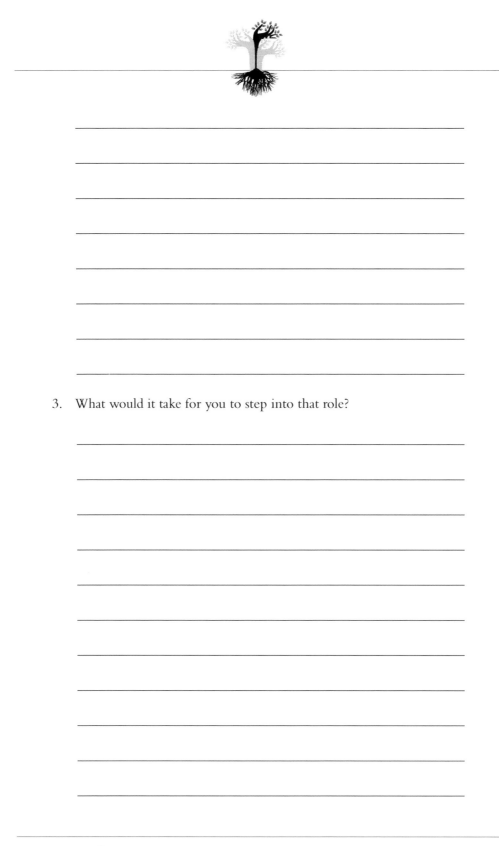

_____

_____

_____

_____

_____

_____

_____

3. What would it take for you to step into that role?

_____

_____

_____

_____

_____

_____

_____

_____

_____

_____

_____

CHAPTER 35

WHEN YOU STEP ASIDE, YOU ALLOW SOMEONE ELSE TO STEP INTO A POSITION OF LEADERSHIP

"The best executive is the one who has sense enough to pick good men to do what he wants done, and self-restraint enough to keep from meddling with them while they do it."

THEODORE ROOSEVELT

One of the best managers I ever met had a simple yet effective approach to management:

He said his staff didn't work for him; he worked for them.

He believed a manager's role is to make direct reports successful—to provide direction, resources, and coaching—and then get out of the way so they can thrive. He had discovered that being the leader of the group required him to shift in three ways: (1) how he defined his role, (2) the skills he used at work, and (3) his sources of satisfaction.

The transition was hard but well worth it, because when his staff was successful, so was he. They had better results, they made more money for the company, and there was less complaining and more individual accountability.

Some managers struggle with delegation, often because of ego, a need for control, or not understanding that their role is to make a connection, engage people's hearts and minds in the work, and provide direction and feedback to align effort with results. They have trouble trusting staff to figure things out or try new things.

Ultimately, if they overcome this struggle, these managers discover that stepping aside and allowing people to step up is a win for everyone:

- Employees learn new skills and have greater job satisfaction.
- The organization has stronger bench strength.
- The manager can take on other responsibilities and experience fewer hassles by letting go of the need to micro-manage others.

GOOD QUESTIONS

1. Think about a time when you could have stepped aside and didn't—at work, in a project, or in a volunteer or community role. What was that about?

    _____

    _____

    _____

    _____

    _____

    a) How did that help or hinder the project or task?

    _____

    _____

    _____

    _____

    _____

    b) What impact did it have on the other person or people involved?

    _____

    _____

    _____

    _____

2. What is one thing you are doing now—at work, in a project, or in a volunteer or community role—where you could step aside and allow some else to step up?

_____

_____

_____

_____

_____

a) What would you gain? What would you lose? What would it mean to the other person and to the organization?

_____

_____

_____

_____

_____

b) What would it take for you to do that?

_____

_____

_____

_____

_____

GOOD THINGS
for Your Professional Life

CHAPTER 36

NETWORKING IS ABOUT BUILDING CONNECTIONS, NOT COLLECTING BUSINESS CARDS

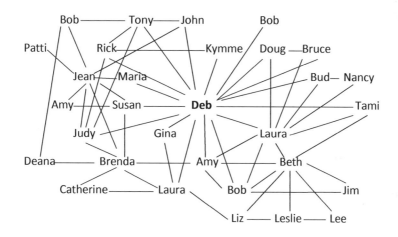

A personal networking map shows how people are connected to each other. Although I am personally connected to each of the individuals involved in *Good Things for a Full Life*, this map—showing my book team and those who have contributed features or testimonials—illustrates how we are connected through and to each other.

I occasionally attend networking events with my friend Leslie. Since we both have full and busy lives, we view networking events as a way to spend time together and enhance our relationships in the larger business community.

But Leslie and I don't just show up and have a good time. We strategize. We select events that are of interest to both of us. We research who else will attend. We decide with whom we want to connect and why. And we plan how we will "work the room."

Of course we have fun. Better yet, we make connections with people who can—and often do—become viable business colleagues.

True networking is about building lasting, reciprocal relationships, where both people commit to share resources and knowledge over time. It means developing partnerships where both parties have expertise and ideas to give.

This is entirely different from attending a business event in order to get something—particularly a stack of business cards, a list of job opportunities, or a slew of new business leads. Enter a room with that focus, and you may meet a lot of people and shake a lot of hands. But I doubt you will receive many follow-up calls.

So map your plan. Attend the event with a networking buddy. And then before you enter that networking event, challenge yourself to meet others purely to see what your shared future might hold. This takes time and openness to the possibilities relationships can bring. And it means focusing more on what you can give than what you can get.

GOOD QUESTIONS

1. What do you have to offer other people? Who might be interested in what you have to offer?

    _____

    _____

    _____

    _____

    _____

    _____

    _____

2. What are you looking to learn or do, and who might be able to help you learn or do that?

    _____

    _____

    _____

    _____

    _____

    _____

3. How can you connect with the people you identified in your answers to those first two questions?

_____

_____

_____

_____

_____

_____

_____

_____

4. Who could be your networking partner, to join in preparing for and attending a networking event in this spirit of building connections, rather than collecting business cards?

_____

_____

_____

_____

_____

_____

GOOD THINGS
for Your Professional Life

CHAPTER 37

KNOW WHAT TO ASK FOR
AND ASK FOR MORE

Not On Sale
by Gina Flaig

The executive who headed our department was a former attorney. I knew this. She knew that I had a penchant for compliance and executing on work. She needed to know what, exactly, she should be losing sleep over: what needed attention to ensure sustained compliance.

I was offered a role to work with a small team to manage a critical project, and I was uniquely qualified to be a part of the solution. The role came with an increase in salary, but no consideration for a higher bonus target or anything else.

I knew I would need additional resources to accomplish the work: a full-time analyst, BlackBerry, secured office area, etc. I knew to ask for it all and then wait for the full "yes" to come back. Because when I said "yes," the window would close on my opportunity to ask for anything else. I also knew the project was at risk if I wasn't part of the solution, but I was fully prepared to walk away if I didn't get it all. I have never been "on sale." I was already in another role, where I could stay if need be.

My stomach churned as the person who would be my manager phoned the vacationing department head to get approval for all of my requests. I stayed in the discomfort and let it play out.

What happened? Everything was approved. Check. Project completed on time. Check. Respect and trust of leadership. Check. Three promotions for me over the next three years. Check.

Not long ago, I was in the market for a new car. This was an important first for me: the first time I would be the primary negotiator—a role my husband was more than happy to relinquish—and the first time we would buy a luxury sedan that didn't need to be family-friendly. Our new car needed to be comfortable for urban driving as well as occasional trips to visit family out of state.

I found a car I wanted. Even more, I wanted this car at a good price. So I reached out to my brother-in-law, John, for advice. John worked as a car sales manager for many years, so he is well versed in the negotiations that take place in the dealer's show room. He had my back.

John guided me through research and preparing my position, and then urged me to check in with him while in discussion with the dealership. So, in the middle of the negotiation, I called John to give him a status report.

"I asked for ten percent off list price," I said. "The salesperson told me she can give me an eight percent discount, but not ten percent."

John listened patiently, then answered: "Deb, I can hear hesitation and resignation in your voice. You sound like you are ready to give in." (He was right.) "If I can hear it, the salesperson can hear it, too."

What he said next surprised me.

"Originally, you asked for ten percent off. You need to go back and ask for more."

John coached me on how to position my request for more. Following his direction, I secured a free ten-thousand-mile service visit, the cost of which was equivalent to the additional two percent discount—the gap between my original request and her first counter-offer.

Sure, John was my secret weapon. But there were other reasons I succeeded in this negotiation:

1. I had done my homework. I knew the value of that car in my area, what I was willing to spend, and how to position my case. I knew what to ask for.
2. I stayed firm in my position.
3. I asked for more.

Whenever I am hesitant to ask for more, I think back on that experience. What if I hadn't asked for anything off the list price? I would have felt like I had been cheated. Every time I drove the car, I would have regretted paying full price.

Part of this lesson is about value—what is of value to both parties and how to position your case so you can get the most value for yourself and for the other party. That requires research and being open to additional outcomes.

And always ask for more. The worst possible response is "no." But you'll never know unless you ask.

GOOD QUESTIONS

1. How do you prepare for a negotiation?

_____

_____

_____

_____

_____

_____

_____

_____

_____

2. Think about an upcoming negotiation. What is of value to you? What does the other party value? What potential obstacles might keep you from getting what you want?

_____

_____

_____

_____

_____

_____

_____

3. If the other party won't meet your original request, how can you ask for more? How can you enable the other party to say yes?

_____

_____

_____

_____

_____

_____

_____

CHAPTER 38

ALWAYS HAVE A BACK-UP PLAN

"Another way to be prepared is to think negatively. Yes, I'm a great optimist. But, when trying to make a decision, I often think of the worst-case scenario. I call it "the eaten by wolves factor." If I do something, what's the most terrible thing that could happen? Would I be eaten by wolves? One thing that makes it possible to be an optimist is if you have a contingency plan for when all hell breaks loose. There are a lot of things I don't worry about, because I have a plan in place if they do."

RANDY PAUSCH

You plan for something to happen, and then it doesn't work out. They don't have it in your size. The fundraising campaign falls short. You don't get the job. The medication eases one pain but creates another. There's an accident blocking traffic on your way to work. Your mother doesn't like her.

As one who likes to have a plan, I used to get frustrated when the unexpected messed with my arrangements. I felt stressed and wasted time worrying about what to do next.

Then a wise friend and mentor taught me to have a back-up plan—an approach I could take if my original idea fell through. All you have to do, she said, is envision how you will achieve your objective if the first option doesn't work.

Now, when mapping out a strategy, I always come up with Plan B right along with Plan A. With a back-up plan in place, my stress melts away. I am prepared if things go awry. I've got options.

In addition to relieving stress, creating a back-up plan allows you to see other options, to be flexible and creative about addressing a situation or completing a task. It also helps you anticipate and be realistic about obstacles. Because, as we all know, stuff happens!

"It pays to plan ahead. It wasn't raining when Noah built the ark."

RICHARD C. CUSHING

GOOD QUESTIONS

1. How do you typically react when your best-laid plans fall through? How has that kind of reaction helped or hurt your ability to achieve your objective?

2. Think about a current plan or situation that might not follow the course you intend. What is your back-up plan?

_____

_____

_____

_____

_____

_____

_____

_____

_____

_____

_____

_____

_____

_____

_____

_____

_____

SECTION FOUR

for Your Physical Life

This section addresses your Physical self–
how to nurture and care for your body throughout your full life.

GOOD THINGS
for Your Physical Life

CHAPTER 39

PRACTICE SELF-CARE

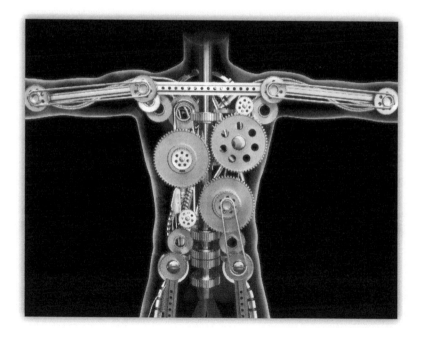

Most of us take great care of our valuable belongings. We keep our cars fueled and tuned. We change furnace filters and have ducts cleaned. We properly store lawn mowers and snow blowers. We've invested money in all this equipment, and we want it to work effectively when we need it.

We care for our assets.

My dad was a dedicated husband and father. He worked very hard to provide for his family. He always put his family's needs before his own. Yet he didn't take good enough care of his most precious asset: his health. He was overweight, rarely exercised, and suffered from high blood pressure and stress. When he died of a massive heart attack at the age of fifty-three, he left my mother and three young children at home.

Losing my father when he was so young had a profound impact on me. He was no longer there to mentor me, he wouldn't know my children, and he wouldn't be able to celebrate the accomplishments of my life. I made a vow to practice self-care so I would be able to live a long and healthy life. And especially since I turned 53, I consider every day a gift—not to be wasted.

Just as we care for the equipment in our lives, we must care for our bodies. Consider your body the engine for the full life you hope to lead, and then care for and maintain that engine so it packs the power you need, when you need it:

- Eat food that is healthy fuel for your body.
- Utilize sleep to restore and replenish your resources.
- Instead of thinking of exercise as a chore, view it as required maintenance.
- Take advantage of regular doctor visits. Consider them tune-ups.

Take good care of your most precious asset, so it will work effectively when you need it.

GOOD QUESTIONS

1. How do you practice self-care for the engine that is your body?

_____

_____

_____

_____

_____

_____

_____

_____

_____

2. How do you sabotage your health? Why do you do that?

_____

_____

_____

_____

_____

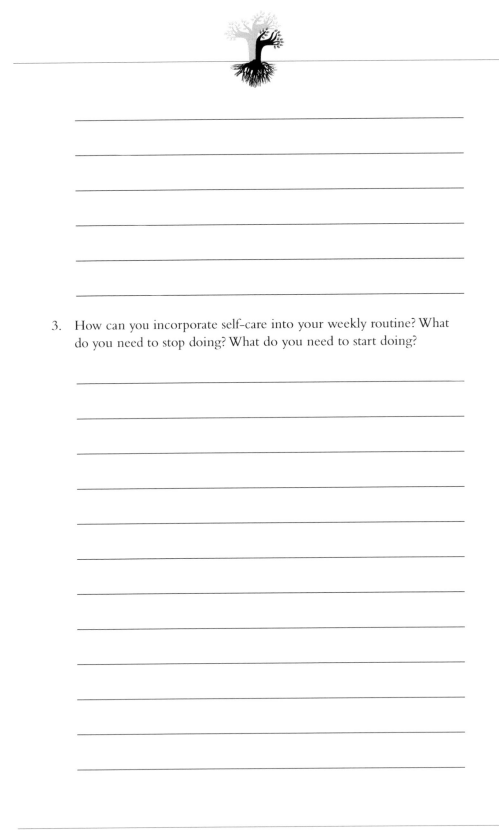

_____

_____

_____

_____

_____

_____

3. How can you incorporate self-care into your weekly routine? What do you need to stop doing? What do you need to start doing?

_____

_____

_____

_____

_____

_____

_____

_____

_____

_____

_____

_____

GOOD THINGS
for Your Physical Life

CHAPTER 40

DESPITE YOUR BEST INTENTIONS, STUFF HAPPENS ...

Tamara's Way
by Tamara K. Fay

I have always felt at my best when I am in control, taking charge, and managing according to Tamara's Way. And still, despite my well-considered plans, checklists, ability to organize events, and problem solving skills, things happen that I cannot control. For all my effort and skill in making a plan, everything does not go according to that plan.

A perfect example was when I traveled to Italy to visit my oldest daughter, who was studying abroad. Naturally, I carefully planned this trip—not only for myself but also for several friends I invited to join me for a week. I had the place, the details, and everything all planned. All they had to do was arrive.

My dear friend Deb took me up on the offer.

The week before she arrived, I had the opportunity to experience Italy. First, I tried it Tamara's Way: planning what I would see, where I would visit, and so on. Before long I discovered, out of necessity, another way: the Italian Way. In this foreign country, circumstances—like train strikes, buses not running according to the published schedule, and museums closed for no reason—challenged me to exercise flexibility and modify my plans like never before.

By the time Deb arrived a week later, I had a new mindset: "Whatever happens, I cannot change it, do anything about it, or fix the problems. It's Italy!"

So, for the rest of the trip, when things did not go according to plan (which happened a lot), I would turn to Deb and say, "It's Italy!" This phrase has stayed with us, even as we navigate our full lives in the U.S. When things don't go as planned, we remind each other to go with the flow—just like we did in Italy.

When something unexpected happens, we are likely taken aback and resistant—especially when the unexpected feels like a negative disruption in our plans. Like a tire in a hole so deep it can't get traction, we stop rolling.

While writing this book, I was diagnosed with an auto-immune disorder. The condition is manageable, not life threatening. But it has already altered my lifestyle and will mean lifelong commitment to certain changes in my diet and daily routines.

Since I have always taken such good care such of myself, I was shocked and had a hard time absorbing the fact that I would have physical limitations and would need to make adjustments in my full life. Because I've always been strong and capable of handling anything that came my way, it was hard to accept that things would be different going forward. I walked around in a daze for quite awhile and spent time researching the disorder, trying to figure out what my future would hold.

Finally, I accepted a "new normal" and set about choosing the way I will think and act from now on. The you-can-do-it voice inside me said, "Deb, this is how it is now. You may as well get in front of this thing and make it work for you."

So I've been exploring ways to continue my favorite activities—swimming, tending my gardens, learning to play the piano, coaching and consulting with my clients, writing, and so much more—while adding important self-care regimens. And it's working! While I have to listen to my body more carefully and accept that I can't operate at warp speed like in the past, I'm getting better at pacing myself and embracing this new chapter in my full life.

Stuff happens. When it does, you just have to get out of the hole and roll with it.

GOOD QUESTIONS

1. How do you react when stuff happens to you? What's that about?

_____

_____

_____

_____

_____

_____

_____

_____

_____

_____

_____

_____

_____

_____

_____

_____

2. How can you shift your thinking so you can "roll with it?"

_____

_____

_____

_____

_____

_____

_____

_____

_____

_____

_____

_____

_____

_____

_____

_____

_____

CONTRIBUTORS

Bruce Andresen

Bruce Andresen manages Steve's Gym/Elkhart Martial Arts, having practiced the martial arts for fifty years. He has received numerous honors, including two Black Belt of the Year awards. He is a certified Tae Kwon Do official with the Amateur Athletic Union, as well as a coach. His interests include travel, fishing, singing, working with kids, and community service. He is especially proud of his work with the Muscular Dystrophy Association, Relay for Life, Santa's Pantry, and the Pay it Forward Movement. He lives with his family and three cats in Indiana, where they spend their time actively involved in a full life.

Doug Andresen

Doug Andresen is known and respected for many things: as a musician, singer and budding guitarist; as a black belt in Aiki and Kenpo Jujitsu; as a dog trainer—a discipline he says would have helped him be a better father; as a strong and caring manager; as a guy who can fix or build just about anything; and as a beloved husband, father, brother, uncle, and "Paw-Paw" to his two grandsons. Most of all, Doug wants to enjoy life—to LIVE, not coast into obscurity, and to mean something to others.

Judy Oliver Busby

Before launching Busby TEAM Consulting, Inc., Judy Busby held leadership roles in the transportation, consulting, publishing, and medical device industries. A life-long learner, she holds an MBA from St. Joseph's University, an M.S. of Management and Organizational Behavior from Benedictine University, and a B.S. in Business Logistics from Penn State University. Judy is especially proud to be a two-time Division I National Champion and field hockey and lacrosse All-American. She and her childhood friend, having played together for more than ten years, were recently inducted into their high school sports Hall of Fame. Judy and her husband Art split their time between Illinois and Arizona, where they maintain an active lifestyle that includes biking, hiking, golfing, and traveling. They look forward to sharing tips on living a full life with new grandson Travis. She is especially thankful for mentoring and guidance from Deb, whose wisdom has helped Judy become a better daughter, wife, aunt, friend, and grandmother. Judy can be reached at busbyteamconsulting.com.

Tamara Fay

Tamara Fay is a consultant and owner of Tamara K Fay Training, LLC, a management training company specializing in leadership development, customer, and career services for more than 25 years. Her full life includes family, work, golf, and exercising. Tamara's accomplishments include running her own business while raising four great children of whom she is most proud. She and her husband recently moved back to the western suburbs of Chicago. She holds a B.S. degree from Bradley University. Tamara has enjoyed golfing with Deb for more than twenty years, and she considers Deb a special and dear friend.

Gina Flaig

Gina Flaig has worked in human resources for almost twenty years, having served at various companies including Sony Electronics, Inc. and United Airlines. Originally from Iowa, Gina has lived in the Chicago area since graduating from Buena Vista University with a B.A. in Psychology. Her full life includes working full time and raising two sweet boys, Owen and Tyler, with her husband Mark and their dog, Ben. Gina enjoys a good cup of coffee and her local library. She is currently challenging herself to get more involved in social media. Gina is proud of her uncompromising drive to make decisions that align with her "gut" and then let life unfold. You can find her on LinkedIn.

Deana Gelino

Deana Gelino, currently a Senior Manager in US Operations at McDonald's USA, has been a part of the McDonald's system for more than ten years, with roles in supplier relationship management both within the company and within the McDonald's supplier community. Born and raised in Chicago, Deana now lives in the city's western suburbs. She has a B.S. in Business from Benedictine University. She is blessed with a supportive husband and fun, energetic, ten-year-old triplet boys who keep her focused on what's important every day. Some seek work-life balance; Deana is committed to work-life choice.

Bud Hornell

Bud Hornell was born and raised in Pittsburgh, Pennsylvania. After graduating from Mt. Lebanon High School, he matriculated to Rensselaer Polytechnic Institute and earned a degree in Metallurgical Engineering. He served in the Navy for four years as a carrier-based jet fighter pilot. While in the Navy he married Glorya Matthews, and they embarked on a life together that later included four children. A succession of jobs followed, with the family accompanying Bud from Pittsburgh to Boston, where he received an MBA from Boston College; to Columbus, Ohio; and then to Elkhart, Indiana. Bud and Glorya moved for the last time to Ft. Myers, Florida, where they enjoyed retirement together until Glorya's death in 2012—after 57 years of love and companionship. Bud still lives in Ft. Myers, where he's doing his best to enjoy this next exciting chapter of life.

Nancy Hoying

Nancy Hoying has worn many hats in her life: human resources manager, training and organizational consultant, wife, mother of three, aunt, philanthropist, friend, and more. Nancy lives in the northern suburbs of Chicago, where she juggles the activities of parenting three beautiful and active children. She enjoys living by the beach, adventure travel with her family, and family dinners where everyone likes what she cooks. Nancy is Deb's sister-in-law and beloved aunt to Deb's children.

Brenda Knapp

As President of Knapp Development Group, Brenda Knapp helps leaders improve their performance by increasing their emotional intelligence and communication expertise. A graduate of The Second City training center, Brenda always brings a sense of humor and playfulness to her interactions, whether in business or with friends and family. Before communication and leadership consulting, Brenda spent fifteen years in advertising and publishing. Her full life includes a wonderful husband, three fantastic teenage children, friends, her dear eighty-nine-year-old father, and a sweet Portuguese Water Dog (together, they are a therapy team to the hospice community). A graduate of Indiana University in English and Telecommunications, Brenda describes herself as a perpetual liberal arts student who is always looking to enrich her full life. An avid reader, runner, and aspiring yogi, Brenda has had the pleasure and privilege of being mentored by Deb in their work with WOMEN Unlimited. "Deb saw talents in me that I didn't know I had, and for that I will always be grateful ... plus she makes me laugh a lot!"

Catherine Lanucha

Catherine C. Lanucha is Deputy Managing Editor of Digital Products for Sun-Times Media, having held various digital leadership roles in the media industry over the past sixteen years. Her full life includes raising three children, scouring social media, nurturing a newly sprouted green thumb, and transforming the media industry. She lives with her family and two schnauzers in the Chicago suburbs.

Kymme Lightfoot

After twenty-three years in various leadership roles within corporate learning and development departments, Kymme Lightfoot is now President of KDL & Associates, where she works with clients one-on-one or in groups—helping them increase productivity, efficiency, and work/life balance and moving them toward achieving personal and professional goals. Kymme is especially proud of feedback she receives from clients when they achieve their goals, whether they succeed at leaving work before 6:00 p.m. or create and execute a strategic plan. Kymme holds a B.S. in Secondary Education and an M.A. in Instructional Design and Management and Human Resources from The Ohio State University. Her full life includes her husband Michael, three kids, two dogs, and various other pets that may change by publication. They live in the northwest suburbs of Chicago. Deb and Kymme have been friends and worked as often as possible together since 1989. Kymme considers Deb a trusted partner and is honored to be a part of this collaborative process. You can connect with Kymme on LinkedIn.

Maria Moore

Maria Moore has more than twenty years of experience in healthcare, having held leadership positions in operations, research, academic medical centers, technology, client relationship management, implementation, program/project management, and C-suite presentations. Maria's full life includes focusing on maintaining a spiritual connection, sharing with extended family, managing a focused career, travel, music, gardening, baking, and a thriving artistic passion for jewelry design. She lives in the Chicagoland area where she can watch her favorite sports: Illinois politics, da Bears, and da Bulls.

Beth Nyland

Thanks in part to a living room conversation over tea with Deb, Beth Nyland is enjoying a full life teeming with good things. She is founder and principal consultant of Spencer Grace LLC, a creative communications consultancy—as well as a wife, mother of six, writer, editor, poet, teacher, coach, singer, reader, occasional exerciser, and wine lover. Beth firmly believes "creative business writing" need not be an oxymoron. Her writing style features everyday words, active verbs, clear examples, and a sense of humor—the same approach she recommends to her clients and students. Her goal is to put forth writing that reaches and involves people so they believe, understand, and do what's needed for an organization to succeed. As Deb's writing coach and editor of this book, she hopes *Good Things for a Full Life* will move you to do what you need to succeed. You can find Beth's consulting website at spencergrace.com and her personal blog at bethnyland.com.

Bob Sitze

Church Consultant Bob Sitze spends his semi-retirement days noodling and writing about the applications of brain science, complexity theory, and organizational development to the life of congregations. His several books include the coming e-volume, *Simple Enough: A Companion Along the Way* (Alban Institute), which helps readers pursue simpler lifestyles. His own life is filled with volunteering, personal correspondence with cherished friends, and reading/writing across the spectrum of current research and social critique. Bob holds a B.S. in Education from Concordia Teachers College and an M.S. in Education from Indiana University. With his wife Chris, Bob lives and works in the western suburbs of Chicago.

John Weaver

During the past twenty-five years, John Weaver has held a variety of leadership positions in the metals and executive search sectors with Alcoa and Russell Reynolds Associates. Now, he is a Managing Partner with Intrepid Consulting Group (intrepidcg.com)—a Chicago-based executive search and assessment firm. In addition to building a small business, John's life includes travel, red wine, good friends, and a little golf. He and his wife Cindy are particularly proud of their three adult children and daughter-in-law: Mike, Allayne, Chrissy, and JJ. John holds a bachelor's degree from Michigan State University and an MBA from Northwestern University's Kellogg School of Management. He and Cindy live in the western suburbs of Chicago with Little Dog (the cat) and Charlie (the real dog). John met Deb through her work with WOMEN Unlimited, and he is honored to be her friend.

Laura Hornell Yudys

Laura Yudys is a Registered Dietitian at Northwestern Memorial Hospital in Chicago, where she specializes in surgery and gastroenterology. She holds a B.S. degree in Food Science and Human Nutrition from The University of Illinois at Urbana-Champaign and an M.S. in Nutrition and Wellness from Benedictine University. Her full life includes movie marathons with her husband, culinary adventures with her friends, laughing with her family, and long runs with her very energetic Jack Russell Terrier. As Deb's oldest daughter, she believes her full life was made possible partly through her mom's unending support, encouragement, and love.

SOURCES

BOOKS AND NEWSPAPERS *(in order of reference in this book)*

Page 5   "Oxford American Desk Dictionary and Thesaurus" (2nd edition).
            Edited by Erin McKean. 2005.
Page 12   "Cosmos" by Carl Sagan. October 1985.
Page 77   "Mom, daughter receiving degrees from Benedictine" by
            Christopher Placek for "Daily Herald." May 16, 2011.
Page 97   "Simple Abundance: A Daybook of Comfort and Joy" by Sara Ban
            Breathnach. September 2009.
Page 98   "Fierce Conversations: Achieving Success at Work & in Life, One
            Conversation at a Time" by Susan Scott. January 2004.
Page 136   "Primal Leadership: Realizing the Power of Emotional Intelligence"
            by Daniel Goleman, Richard E. Boyatzis, and Annie McKee.
            January 2004.

QUOTATIONS *(in order of reference in this book)*

Page 43   Mahatma Gandhi's quote sourced from BestSpirituality.com.
Page 59   Clark Moustakas's quote from "Sacred Simplicities: Meeting the
            Miracles in Our Lives" by Lori Knutson. October 2004.
Page 102   Katherine Mansfield's quote from "Talks with Katherine Mansfield"
            by A. R. Orage. November 1924.
Page 111   Dan Schawbel's quote from his website: PersonalBrandingBlog.com.
Page 127   Colin Powell's quote from "It Worked for Me: In Life and
            Leadership" by Colin Powell with Tony Koltz. May 2012.
Page 135   Plato's quote sourced from ThinkExist.com.
Page 144   Gilda Radner's quote from "It's Always Something" by Gilda Radner.
            July 2000.
Page 147   Theodore Roosevelt's quote sourced from BrainyQuote.com.
Page 159   Randy Pausch's quote from "The Last Lecture" by Randy Pausch
            with Jeffrey Zaslow. April 2008.
Page 160   Richard C. Cushing's quote sourced from QuoteLand.com.

16893555R00102

Made in the USA
Charleston, SC
16 January 2013